Praise for *Your Destiny Switch*

*"If you are ready to make your destiny
all it can be, read Peggy's book—<u>now!</u>"*

— **Mark Victor Hansen,** the co-creator of the #1
New York Times best-selling series *Chicken Soup for the Soul*®

*"Your Destiny Switch exposes what it takes to be rich—in
every sense of the word. You will discover amazing and simple
strategies to finally live a life of true opulence, joy, and love."*

— **Dean Graziosi,** the author of *Totally Fulfilled*

*"Wow! Just when you think you've seen it all, along comes a book
that awakens your heart, soul, and mind. An inspiring masterpiece!"*

— **Joe Vitale, Ph.D.,** the author of *The Attractor Factor*

*"Is it true that you can have everything you ever ask for, and
that your emotions are the key to achieving your highest dreams?
In Your Destiny Switch, the answer lies waiting like a wondrous
gift tucked beneath the brightest tree you've ever seen.
Unwrap it and its secrets will be yours. It really is true."*

— **James Twyman,** the author of
Emissary of Light and *Emissary of Love*

*"Some people believe they are destined for a life of
continuous struggle. However, if you have a desire to
live a more empowering life, creating an abundance of joy and
easily attracting success to you, then I urge you to read this book."*

— **David Riklan,** the founder of **SelfGrowth.com,**
the #1 self-improvement Website, and the creator
of the *101 Great Ways to Improve Your Life* series

YOUR DESTINY

SWITCH

Hay House Titles of Related Interest

YOUR DESTINY

SWITCH

Master Your Key Emotions, and Attract the Life of Your Dreams!

PEGGY McCOLL

HAY HOUSE, INC.
Carlsbad, California
London • Sydney • Johannesburg
Vancouver • Hong Kong • New Delhi

To you, the reader.

It is my honor and privilege to serve.

CONTENTS

FOREWORD

Very few people I know are living the lives that they want to live. Most are working for something, striving for something, or struggling to get where they want to be. Some people are dragging themselves through life, just getting by. Others are doing reasonably well but are still not living the life that they really *want* to live. They may have gotten lucky—may have "caught a wave"—but their lives are not bringing them what they truly desire.

It is amazing how few people understand that life was never meant to be this way . . . and that it doesn't *have* to be this way. Many people simply settle for finding some level of contentment with their "lot in life." They've long ago given up on their dreams. And most people never consider the possibility that life is something they can control. But it is.

It *is.*

Life is not only something you *can* control—it is something you *are* controlling, every day. If the first part of that sentence is a surprise, the second one has to be a blockbuster. Both parts are true. And those 16 words can change your life.

Consider the book you are holding in your hands. How did it get there? By what set of circumstances did it come to be placed before your eyes right now? Do you think that you had anything to do with it? Well, of course you did. It was you who picked it up; it was you who started reading it. But I'm talking about all this at a deeper level. What *made* you pick it up? What *caused* you to start reading it? How did it come into your possession to begin with? There are millions of books in the world. *Millions.* How did this particular one happen to be called to you—or you to it—just now?

I am going to tell you how.

Somewhere in your mind—perhaps in the farthest reaches, but somewhere in your mind—you held a thought, and that thought has been backed by emotion. The thought you've held is: *I want my life to change.* And the emotion that you have backed it up with is an earnest yearning . . . a very deep, real, earnest yearning.

Emotion is to your thoughts what gold is to your money. Money without gold behind it is worthless. A thought without emotion behind it is just data. If you think a thought and back it up with emotion, it becomes a creative force.

Many people think that emotion is bad. How many times have you heard someone say, "Now, now, don't get all *emotional*"? Even positive emotion is very often discouraged: "Hey, hey, calm down. Don't get so *excited.*"

Yet emotion is what put this book into your hands. Your yearning placed it there.

Believe it.

This book is going to bring you all the tools you will ever need to switch your destiny. There's only one question left now: Will you use this book? Will you *heed* it as well as *read* it? If your decision is yes, you are on your way to the life for which you have yearned.

I am not trying to tell you that everything is going to be easy from now on. In fact, using the tools that are offered here requires discipline. It takes determination. But, given those, you cannot fail to succeed in bringing yourself a level of happiness, peace, and sufficiency greater than any you have known.

It is important to understand, as a basis for moving now into this reading, that life is not happening *to* you; it is happening *through* you.

How? Ah, yes, that is the question, isn't it. . . .

You are holding the answer in your hands.

This may be the most important book you have ever read. I am grateful to Peggy McColl for having written it. I believe you will be, too. So hurry and finish it, and begin applying its principles.

It is not too much to say, as you hold this book in this moment, that your destiny is in your hands.

— **Neale Donald Walsch**
Ashland, Oregon

INTRODUCTION

Four Epiphanies

For most of my early years, I was living in a prison and I didn't know it. When I think about the girl I was and who I am today, it's as if they're completely different people. It took many years, a lot of pain, and four epiphanies for me to make the journey from a confused, unhappy teen to a self-assured, contented woman in charge of her emotions and her destiny.

Today I'm a consultant and what I call a *Goal-Achieving Mentor*, inspiring individuals, professional athletes, and organizations to connect to their passion, create goals, and reach their maximum potential. I've been doing this work for 25 years, and the insights and skills that I've acquired have allowed me to assist hundreds of people in creating the life they want to live. But I wasn't always enthusiastic, optimistic, and at peace with myself. As a teenager and young adult, I was living in a prison of negativity and had no idea that the key to escaping it was to harness the power of my emotions and use it to create the life I wanted for myself.

Over time, I discovered that as overwhelming as emotions may seem, we have the power to manage them, just as we have the potential to create our own destiny. I realized that it's as if we each have a Destiny Switch, a board of dimmer switches, each of which controls an emotional pairing—such as happiness versus sadness—and we have the ability to move those levers up and down, creating or enhancing positive feelings and turning down the volume on negative, destructive ones. However, like many people, I started out thinking that my emotions were controlled by people and situations outside of myself. I needed to discover my power and learn how to use it.

Epiphany 1: You Cannot Escape from a Prison
Unless You Know You Are in One

Back in my teenage years, I was sad, lonely, and insecure. I was imprisoned by my dark feelings, and like many troubled people, I drank because it made me feel better—temporarily. For a few short hours, the alcohol would allow me to blot out my pain and experience confidence and happiness, but of course the next day all my negative feelings came back full force, and I discovered that my self-assurance had once again dissipated. I had no idea how I might find a more permanent solution to my woes.

For several years, I was angry and depressed that no one was showing up to permanently fix my life for me. I was too immature to take responsibility for my choices, and I blamed everyone for my problems and my dark feelings. The longer I waited for somebody to swoop in and rescue me, the more unmanageable my life became, the more frightened and frustrated I grew, and the worse I felt about myself. I spent most of my days feeling miserable, with no idea that I had the power to change my feelings and my life.

My lowest point came one day when I was 17. For nearly three years, I'd been dating Dave, a popular football player at school. I'd been as surprised as I was happy when he asked me out for the first time, since I couldn't imagine why he wanted to be with me (my sense of self-worth was very low). Dave treated me with warmth and affection and soon asked me to be his girlfriend.

Knowing that he loved me helped me feel some hope that my painful feelings would one day be completely replaced by happiness and a sense of well-being. I didn't realize that only *I* could create those emotions for myself. And now Dave was telling me that he wanted to "take a break" from our relationship and that he'd started seeing another girl.

I already felt terrible about myself (and when I think about it, that's probably the reason he broke up with me in the first place), and it seemed as if life just wasn't worth living. I was sure that I'd never laugh or smile or feel joyful again. I assumed, as many people do, that happiness is a state that we magically fall into when good things happen to us. It didn't occur to me that it's something we create for ourselves and I could feel content even when I had challenges in my life.

As the years went by, I dated many men and enjoyed several long-term relationships, but these romances never gave me any lasting sense of security or tranquility. I needed constant reassurance from my boyfriends and obsessed over whether they were cheating on me. Eventually, no matter how promising the relationship had seemed initially, it would end, sabotaged by my insecurity.

Since men couldn't give me the happiness and peace I sought, I tried to get it through working and making money. As a teenager with a part-time job, I'd loved having the money to purchase the most stylish pair of $50 jeans. Having spending power helped me feel good about myself. By the time I was out of high school, I had a job doing sales for a computer manufacturer, and I was donning a business suit and talking to customers about the superiority of the company's product. I relished having influence over their decisions while earning a steady paycheck.

But the job wasn't going as smoothly as it could have. I was very frustrated—everything about the company I worked for and its managers was "wrong." I thought that their attitudes stunk, and I hated being told what to do. I was unhappy and blamed *them.* I got nothing out of the performance-improvement programs they had me take, since I couldn't see how any of the difficulties at work might be caused by me. I jumped from department to department, seeking better co-workers and assignments, but nothing seemed to fix my attitude or unhappiness.

Once again, I was looking outside myself for the answer to my problems. I felt that if I could just arrange the ideal job situation, the perfect boyfriend, and the right everything else, I'd feel wonderful about my life and wouldn't have to suffer insecurity, anger, jealousy, or sadness. I couldn't yet see that wherever I went, I was taking my misery along with me, creating a prison for myself.

Then one day the company hired a motivational speaker named Bob Proctor for our annual corporate morale-boosting event. I found myself sitting in the front row. (Today that's normal behavior for me, but it certainly wasn't back then, when I hated being noticed unless I was making a point of being visible.) As I listened to Bob speak, many of the things he mentioned started to make sense to me. I was awed by his brilliance and wisdom, and I experienced my first epiphany when he said the following:

**"You cannot escape from a
prison unless you know you are in one."**

His words seemed to reverberate throughout my body, and I felt myself buzzing with excitement. It suddenly dawned on me that I truly was living in a prison—a dark, cold prison of dreadful feelings—and I was the one who'd created it.

My negative emotions weren't extreme or out of control, but I was plagued by a continual sense of insecurity that kept me feeling small and inconsequential. I lacked faith in myself, and I was constantly afraid of failure (which was at the root of my blustering about the arrogance of others at work). Deep down, I had no confidence. Sure, I had a good job, but I'd simply followed the opportunities that opened up to me, so I didn't feel as if I'd been responsible for my success. I didn't dare dream about what I really wanted to do. I was afraid that if I made a goal and didn't reach it, the disappointment would be soul crushing.

As for relationships, my attitude was "Been there, done that," and I was convinced that love equaled pain. No wonder I was just chugging away at my job—it was the one aspect of my life I felt control over, and even then, I was secretly terrified of messing up somehow. I had no sense of purpose or destiny, just a lingering anxious feeling that I'd better make the best of whatever my life was and hope that the joy I was seeking would magically appear someday.

With no vision and no sense of my own destiny, I was indeed living in a prison. Bob Proctor's words resonated with me, and I mulled them over in my mind again and again. One day while I was standing downtown on a busy street near the office where I worked, the clouds suddenly parted, and bright rays of sunshine warmed my face. I had this overwhelming sensation that I was going to do something big— something that would make a huge, positive difference in the lives of thousands of people who, just like me, were unhappy and confused. I didn't have a clue as to what that "something" would be, but now that I knew I was in a prison and that a better path awaited me, I was determined to break out of my confinement and create a happy life.

I realized that I held the key to my prison door: managing the destructive emotions that were weighing me down and holding me back. I knew that if I could do this, I'd find the confidence, enthusiasm, and optimism that would propel me forward. I didn't know how to control my feelings, but it was clear to me that learning to do so was my central challenge.

I was starting to recognize that neither my employer nor my boyfriend had the power to create a happier life for me. I was the only one who could shape my destiny . . . and so my self-help journey began.

Epiphany 2: Knowledge Alone Is Not Enough

I stuck to my commitment to take responsibility for my emotions, my choices, and my life. I wanted to fulfill my destiny in this world, the calling that had come to me that day when the clouds broke. I decided that it was my job to find out how to fix my problems on my own.

My life was changing in many positive ways: I was the national marketing director for a major computer company, I was accumulating wealth, and I had many terrific friends and a pretty good life—but that wasn't enough. I was passionately studying self-improvement. "Passionately" may be an understatement, because I dug so deeply into the process that I became a self-help addict. I attended every motivational seminar that I could, eagerly waiting in line to grab a front-row seat and rushing out to buy all the inspirational books and tapes that the speakers recommended. Small public libraries stock fewer books than I managed to read; I listened to a greater number of audio programs than most recording studios produce; and I attended more seminars than there were hours in a day, traveling extensively to get to all of them. I was spending more on self-help products than most people pay for housing, yet for all my devotion to my cause, it was becoming obvious to me that this endeavor wasn't making me feel contented.

After 11 years of study, I started to have serious doubts about the so-called strategies for achieving happiness and fulfillment. I thought that I should be feeling terrific all the time. My expectations for a permanent state of elation were keeping me from recognizing just how far I'd come, and I began to lose faith and feel frightened and desperate again. One day, I attended a lecture by Bob Proctor, who by now was my favorite motivational speaker. This time I had my second epiphany when he said:

"Knowledge alone is not enough. Only with understanding can real application begin. And that will help bring you to the place you want to be."

This was a true "Aha!" moment. I realized that hearing the insights of all the self-help experts I could find wasn't getting me to wrest control of my life and shape my destiny, because I hadn't internalized their wisdom. I'd written it on sticky notes and in journals, but I wasn't connecting to what they were telling me, so I couldn't truly understand it or apply it to my life. I was too busy congratulating myself for being a seeker of truth to slow down and process what I was taking in. Even the idea that I was in charge of my destiny really hadn't sunk in. Unknowingly, I'd been expecting motivational speakers to do it for me.

As a result of this epiphany, I developed a passion for deeper understanding. I realized that I needed to apply what I'd learned and actually experience the truths that these teachers were imparting to me. I began to think about what they'd taught me about emotions and to look more closely at how I was experiencing my feelings. Why was it so hard for me to stay positive when I knew how important it was to do so? Why did I descend into a pit of anger or self-loathing with such ease? So many things could push my buttons and make me feel negative. Rather than letting my emotions continue to rule my life and imprison me, I decided that it was time for me to search further to figure out why I was at their mercy and what to do about it.

Epiphany 3: It Only Takes a Little Bit of Poison to Kill

By this point, I was married to a wonderful man. All my life, I'd dreamed of having a happy marriage; and Charles was funny, warm, and caring. I felt that I had worked through a lot of my own insecurities and was ready to be a part of a healthy, loving relationship—but I wasn't. Unbeknownst to me, I still had a deeply rooted feeling of unworthiness, so even though I had attracted this terrific man into my life, I was subconsciously sabotaging yet another relationship. I was afraid that if I confronted him about any of the problems in our marriage, he'd get angry and leave me; therefore, I repressed the difficult emotions of fear and low self-worth and pretended everything was fine. He didn't speak up about his needs, and I didn't voice mine.

Again, attending a seminar of Bob Proctor's sparked an epiphany for me. Bob placed two clear glasses on a table, each half full—one with coffee, the other with water. He took a teaspoon of water and stirred it into the glass that held coffee, but I could see no change in it. He mixed in another teaspoonful of water—and another, and another. It wasn't until he'd added several spoonfuls that I began to observe the coffee becoming slightly more transparent. Bob explained that this represented the effect of positive emotions on a person who has a negative state of mind.

As I sat there, I took in his words and tried to apply them to my life. I had to admit that it did take a great deal of positive energy for me to overcome my feelings of anger, sadness, or unworthiness.

Then Bob stirred one teaspoonful of the coffee into the glass of clear water. Instantly, I perceived the liquid changing color. He explained that this is the effect of negativity on a positive mind: It's like a tiny bit of poison. Bob's words became my third epiphany:

"It only takes a little bit of poison to kill."

It was true. While for the most part I felt as if my life was moving forward, each time I experienced something that brought a negative emotion, I immediately returned to that devastated, hopeless feeling I'd experienced when I was a teenager in misery. If someone at work criticized me, or Charles and I had an argument, all my positive feelings vanished—and anger, embarrassment, and unworthiness hijacked me. The smallest bit of poison would kill my positive attitude.

Here I'd convinced myself that all these self-help gurus were living perfect lives, free from any jealousy, anger, or self-doubt, so anytime *I* experienced those negative emotions, I felt bad about myself. Instead of trying to be more positive, I let my toxic feelings dominate my experience, and then I felt guilty and awful for not being more in control of my emotions.

It began to dawn on me that my expectations of myself were completely unrealistic. I started to realize that all the self-help experts weren't trying to tell me that I couldn't experience negativity, but rather that I needed to manage its effect on my life and stop letting it act like a drop of cyanide, destroying my outlook. I needed to develop the habit of learning what I could from my darker feelings before quickly pulling myself out of my negative emotional state and back into a positive one.

After having my third epiphany, I started to apply Bob's words to my life, but it was too late to save my marriage. I'd always been so afraid of my negative feelings that I refused to explore them, and they had acted like a poison within my relationship.

When I look back, I remember that my marriage was filled with love, caring, loyalty, and faithfulness. Still, instead of experiencing gratitude, I felt unworthiness. It wasn't an overwhelming feeling so much as a lingering sense that I didn't deserve happiness. Sadly, within a very short period of time, Charles and I were both so unhappy that our relationship began to unravel. Within four short years, we were divorced and living 20 miles apart. Of course, we both loved our little boy, Michel, deeply and wanted what was best for him more than anything else, so we shared custody. Against all odds, my ex-husband and I created a solid, respectful, loving relationship as co-parents; in fact, we're still friends. But it was sad to realize that our divorce wouldn't have been necessary if I'd only recognized my toxic feelings of unworthiness years earlier.

Epiphany 4: To Have It All, You Have to Be Willing to Give It All Up

My journey of self-discovery continued for a few more years, and I was expanding my sense of myself and my own identity. In many ways, I thought that I was finally starting to feel successful and happy. I had a growing sense of well-being and satisfaction, and I adored being a mother and taking care of my son. I was enjoying my life as a single woman and investing plenty of quality time in my relationship with Michel. In addition, I bought a lovely, beautifully decorated four-bedroom home in a wonderful neighborhood. I was making a good living, earning more and more each year. I sensed that I was on the path to my destiny of helping others.

I was feeling optimistic about life and more secure than ever as I consciously worked on developing a sense of worthiness. I was bravely facing my difficult negative emotions, learning what I could from them and actively choosing to replace them with more positive feelings. However, there was still something missing. As much as I was making progress, I knew that I had the power within me to create so much more.

Financial worries, and fears that I might not find love again, gnawed at me. I didn't know why I was so restless and was experiencing a sense of lack. It didn't occur to me that my emotions were causing me to feel vaguely dissatisfied because they were so subtle that I often didn't recognize them. My positive feelings were there, but it was as if many of them were barely audible and I had to strain to hear them.

I felt that if I tried harder, I could "force" success and take my life to a whole new level, but I quickly found that I wasn't getting where I wanted to go, no matter how hard I worked. Consequently, I held tightly to everything that I achieved while still being consumed by negative thoughts and feelings about what I didn't have. The success I enjoyed led me to want more—I believed that if I just made additional money, I'd be less anxious and more at peace. But the harder I worked to keep what I had and grab for more, the greater the fear I felt.

Then my income began to drop, and I frantically tried to figure out what I was doing wrong professionally. I took some necessary risks to boost business, but what I didn't realize was that by focusing on what I *didn't* want to experience (namely, fear, anxiety, and lack), I was holding myself back from achieving what I *did* want—contentment, calm, and abundance. I tried to believe the spiritual teachers and self-help experts who said that prosperity would be mine if only I'd accept it, but it felt as if I had no control over making more money. I was terrified of losing my business and my home, and I was getting sucked into a whirlpool of negativity. I questioned my self-worth and wondered how I could have the nerve to teach others about being successful. I was dangerously close to losing everything that I'd worked so hard to achieve.

Fortunately, I read a book by Deepak Chopra, *The Seven Spiritual Laws of Success,* that led me to my fourth epiphany:

"To have it all, you have to be willing to give it all up."

I thought about Dr. Chopra's words and tried to apply them to my own life. I knew what he was getting at: I needed to let go of the fear that I would lose myself if I lost my "things." I realized that if I did so, I'd truly be able to stop being so afraid. But did I have the courage to surrender it all?

The truth is that I didn't necessarily have to give up everything I had (I didn't have to relinquish my house, for example), but I understood that I had to be *willing* to give it all up. I had to be prepared to detach from what I owned, because by being attached to situations, I was creating powerful negative feelings. I didn't have faith that no matter what happened around me—regardless of what I might lose—I had the power to control my anxiety and fear and create happiness for myself. I was afraid that if I lost what I had, my destructive emotions would take charge of my life.

I realized that there was no reason to be possessive when it came to my material wealth if I could just have faith that everything in my life could be created again, because I'd created it in the first place. If you have the power to build, you have the power to *re*build. In my head, I trusted that money is just an outward manifestation of the abundance and wealth that's experienced within, but I had to be convinced of that in my heart. I finally understood that laboring to create the things I wanted for myself wasn't nearly as effective as focusing on creating my desired emotions. I didn't have to work or think harder; I needed to forge the positive feelings that were associated with my goals.

If I wanted to be confident, I had to create the *feeling* of confidence, and the universe would respond by helping me succeed. If I hoped to be wealthy, I needed to create a *feeling* of richness and abundance, and the universe would bring me prosperity. I understood that what I co-created might not come in the form I expected. (For instance, maybe I'd draw in new clients, but it would be through an unexpected avenue—or I'd get the money I was seeking not by acquiring additional business, but through another source.) Of course, I had to work to make the most of the opportunities that the universe presented to me, but I now knew that I didn't have to continue to frantically struggle to achieve my goals. I could attract the situations that mirrored my feelings of happiness, abundance, and confidence.

When I began to genuinely believe that I'm more than what I have—that I'm not defined by what I've achieved, and I don't have to point to material goods as evidence of my worthiness—my life started to change dramatically. I created the emotions that I wanted to feel, and the newfound power within me allowed me to grow and prosper as I'd never done before in my life.

The Four Epiphanies and Your Destiny Switch

In the experience of sharing my story and coaching others who've walked a similar path, I find that the four epiphanies I had are continually affirmed:

1. *You cannot escape from a prison unless you know you are in one.* Negative emotions are a prison. Managing them is the key that unlocks the door.

2. *Knowledge alone is not enough.* It must be supplemented with deep understanding and practical application. Positive thoughts only have the power to change your life when they're fueled by positive emotions. Your heart has to truly believe that you can form your own destiny, and you must actively create and turn up the volume on positive feelings in order to achieve the life of your dreams.

3. *It only takes a little bit of poison to kill.* Never underestimate the destructive power of negative emotions. Remember that the antidote to the poison of negativity is positive emotions.

4. *To have it all, you have to be willing to give it all up.* If you feel deserving of it, you can create it; and if you created it once, you can do so again using the power of your positive emotions. There's no need to become attached to situations. No matter what changes in your life, the universe will respond to the call of your positive emotions and bring you what you need and desire . . . in its own time and in its own way.

What became very clear to me through these epiphanies is that feelings are extremely powerful and completely shape our lives and our destinies. The better we're able to recognize our feelings, learn from them, and manage them, the easier it is to live out our purpose and find lasting happiness. I made it my passion to learn about working with emotions, and now I teach others how to harness the force of theirs and take charge of their own destiny.

In these pages, I'll explain the system that I've developed, which will help you identify and balance the powerful emotions that affect your daily life. My hope is that when you've finished reading this book, you'll enthusiastically begin a program of practicing the skills I've taught you, creating the life that you want to live. Whatever you desire—personally, professionally, or financially—you deserve it! I truly believe that you can create it for yourself by taking charge of your emotions.

How to Use This Book to
Manifest the Life You Want to Live

The system I've created for working with your emotions starts with understanding both the power and the nature of emotions. In Part I, I'll help you truly understand the enormous force of your emotions, which I hope will inspire you to want to harness them. I'll also explain what emotions are and why they have so much influence on you.

Part II focuses on understanding the way positive and negative emotions interact and how to work with both types. I'll show you how the visual image of a dimmer switchboard can help you manage your emotions, and I'll explain how you can turn up the volume on empowering, creative emotions and pull yourself out of the negative ones that drag you down. I'll also teach you about specific positive emotions that can benefit you in ways you might never have thought of, along with negative feelings that can be helpful for learning more about yourself but which have to be switched out of quickly if you want to achieve your destiny.

Part III will provide you with more guidance and practical advice on how to use your Destiny Switch. You'll learn Switching Strategies to pull yourself up out of negative feelings quickly, which can be practiced habitually to maintain a positive emotional state overall. I'll also explain how to use several "Illuminators"—exercises that I've found particularly powerful for helping people turn up the light and positivity in their life and dissipate the darkness and negativity. And I'll demonstrate how focusing on four core emotions can assist you in achieving any particular goal.

Too often people will read a self-help book, get enthusiastic about the ideas, and then not follow through with the life-changing actions that they've learned about. Or they'll start a self-improvement regimen, and when an unexpected challenge arises, they'll lose faith in the program instead of working at it more diligently. In Part IV, I'll give you special guidance for difficult times and provide you with the template for a Destiny Planner. This tool will help you stay on track by creating the habit of using Illuminators and Switching Strategies that will allow you to more easily move the levers on your Destiny Switch.

PART I

THE
WORLD
WITHIN YOU

CHAPTER ONE

The Power of Your Emotions

Emotions are incredibly powerful forces. They are able to propel you to achieve your destiny and overcome the most traumatic events, or they can cause you to become immobilized by small setbacks. Life will always present you with surprises, and you can only exert so much control over the world outside you. However, you always—*always*—have the choice to manage and balance your emotions.

It may not seem this way when your strong emotions get the better of you, but you don't have to be at their mercy. You also needn't remain in unhappy situations, unable to move forward because you're convinced that you don't have enough enthusiasm, courage, or determination to get out of your rut and onto the path of your destiny.

It's important to realize that there's no way you can have complete control over your emotions. Everyone has off days, and we all suffer the traumas that are a natural part of life. People die or move away, relationships come to an end, and disappointments occur. There will be times when you experience negative feelings, such as anger or sadness, as well as occasions when your positive ones, including confidence or happiness, aren't as strong as you'd like them to be. Yet when you've developed your ability to balance your emotions, unexpected problems won't knock you off balance as easily, and you'll return more quickly to a positive outlook.

Balanced Emotions

When your emotions are in balance, you probably don't give them much thought. Whatever your situation, you're feeling good. You want to do considerate things and be kind to other people because you're in touch with your highest self and filled with love. You're optimistic about the future, and you aren't looking back at the past with regret. You're content and peaceful, accepting things just the way they are, yet you're also energetic and enthusiastic.

When you don't feel this way, you could think that it's because life has gone awry, but that's not the case. You may miss your exit on the freeway and spend an unexpected 20 minutes doubling back, or you might open your credit-card bill and discover that you've gone way over budget this month, but neither of these experiences has to result in your becoming furious, completely stressed out, or terrified. You do have a choice about the way you feel, as well as how much fear you experience (as opposed to confidence) and your level of joy in relation to sadness.

I've found that when my emotions are in balance, I feel a deep sense of gratitude. I recognize the gifts I have and everything that's wonderful in my life, and I put any problems that I'm experiencing into perspective. I feel compelled to contribute to the world, and my mind becomes filled with positive thoughts. However, when my emotions are out of balance, I focus on what isn't working in my life instead of what is.

Recently, a friend of mine named Renee was driving her seven-year-old son home from school, and she was preoccupied with worry. She had a lot of bills to pay and was having difficulty making money. Her husband had been ill and unable to work, so they'd fallen behind on their mortgage. This was a serious situation that required her attention, but it didn't demand her undivided attention every minute of the day.

As she drove, her son began to chatter away about the changing color of the leaves and how when a maple-leaf seedpod is thrown up into the air, it spins on its way down like a helicopter. Renee barely acknowledged what her son was saying because she couldn't stop thinking about her financial situation.

When she pulled up to a red light, Renee looked over at her son and in a moment of awareness, realized that she was missing out . . . that her constant worrying was preventing her from truly listening and connecting to her child. Worse, she'd made a habit of half listening to him as she internally fretted about her problems. Renee realized that she wanted to snap out of her fear and choose a different emotion. She asked herself, *What else could I feel right now instead of fear or worry?*

Renee had several choices. She could feel:

- Gratitude that she was able to spend time with her son, and that the two of them were close

- Joy as she listened to him talk about what was on his mind

- Curiosity and genuine concern about what his day was like

- Confidence and faith in her ability to handle her financial crisis

In fact, she could experience all these emotions at once if she chose to. She might not be able to let go of her anxiety completely, but she also didn't have to let it dominate her emotions. By allowing her mood to be overwhelmed by worry over one aspect of her life, she was dampening any positive emotions she might feel. Her emotions weren't in balance, and everything seemed dark.

We've all had a moment similar to Renee's in which we realize that whatever emotion we're experiencing, it's not one that makes us feel good. Often our desire to return to feeling better is enough to inspire us to try to change our emotional balance.

Emotions and Destiny

Balancing your emotions is crucial because it allows you to reach your destiny. You have to be able to minimize negativity and raise the volume on those feelings that will most help you.

Many people don't think much about their destiny, and may even be intimidated by the term, mistakenly believing that something as grand as "destiny" is reserved for historical figures, spiritual leaders, and famous people. I firmly believe that every one of us has a destiny, and to discover what it is, we have to connect with what makes us feel the most vibrant and joyful. Then we can harness the power of our emotions to achieve that destiny.

Some people feel that destiny is predetermined, but I agree with Neale Donald Walsch's take on it, which he so beautifully expresses in his book *Conversations with God* (Book 1): "Each soul must choose—*is choosing*—its own destiny this instant." I believe that every one of us makes our own destiny, and we experience it when we find ourselves in a state of contentment and peace, sensing a deep connection to the sacred. One person might experience bliss simply working in his or her flower garden, bringing forth beauty in that small corner of the world. Another might experience it while speaking in front of large crowds, inspiring them with his or her words (while someone else might find this experience about as "blissful" as root canal!).

Your destiny might be as simple as being the neighbor with a ready laugh who always reminds others to find the humor in any experience. In fact, if you look back on the people who've most influenced you, bringing you joy and inspiring you, I'd bet that many of them led very simple lives.

If you're not sure what your destiny is, ask yourself these questions:

- What makes me feel most excited, vibrant, and alive?

- Is there anything I do that I love so much that time just seems to fly?

- Is there a particular activity that puts me most in touch with my spirit and with the sacred?

Keep in mind that your destiny doesn't necessarily define what you do for a living, although it may. If your destiny is to heal others, you might become a surgeon, a psychotherapist, or an acupuncturist—or you could spend your time repairing rifts between other people even as you heal your own emotional wounds. If your destiny is to make other people feel joy and connect with their spirit, you could become a famous entertainer, or you might sing in a church choir.

When you look at how you spend your time, ask yourself: *Does doing this help me achieve my destiny? Does it make me feel in touch with my passion, joy, and spirit . . . or does it take me away from them?* When

I'm following my destiny, I feel bliss—and what's more, I experience success at whatever I choose to do, whether it's helping people publicize their books or being a good parent to my son, Michel, by listening to him and emotionally supporting him as I drive him to hockey practice or fix his dinner.

One thing I've learned about destiny is that trying to define it very narrowly and thinking that it has to unfold in a very specific way, according to a precise timeline, can cause me to feel disappointed or unhappy. I always want to have enough money and resources to help me achieve my destiny of assisting others in understanding themselves more deeply and feeling better about themselves, but I used to be very particular about what those resources should be and when the checks should arrive in my mailbox! I would tie my goals into a timeline: "By next fall, I'll have accomplished such and such," or "By January 1, I'll have X amount of money in the bank."

I'd also try to figure out exactly how I'd reach my goal and then get frustrated or fearful if things didn't turn out precisely as I'd planned. I came to recognize that I could stay true to my destiny yet be open to the many ways in which it might unfold. I also learned to trust in the timing of the universe, rather than panicking if what I desired didn't come to me when I thought it should.

Four years ago, I wanted to start spending more time giving speeches and conducting seminars, but I ended up helping authors publicize their books through the Internet. I'm still achieving my destiny—I'm just doing it in a different form than I'd expected. I can't guarantee that ten years from now I'll be doing the same work, and I know that in a decade Michel will be driving himself wherever he wants to go and making his own meals. He won't need me to take care of him as he does today, but that doesn't mean my destiny will change. I'll just be following different opportunities to nurture my son, just as I may find new ways to help others with their self-growth.

When you're on the road to your destiny, you can sense it. Don't talk yourself out of doing what you're meant to do just because you feel scared for some reason or don't know what turn to make next. It may take a while for your next opportunity to reveal itself. You're never wasting time as long as you're keeping your eyes and your heart open to possibilities for achieving your destiny. You might be learning something crucial to what you'll do in the future.

I know someone who majored in Latin in college much to the amusement of her friends, who thought that it was a useless and impractical field of study. She loved the analytical skills that Latin required, and developing them aided her in being able to understand and design computer-network systems. She now has a job she loves doing just that. In helping other people overcome their fears about technology and instead use it as a tool to do what they want, she feels that she's living out her destiny of making the most of her analytical skills and teaching others how to accomplish their own goals. Now she works part-time because she has children, and she's teaching *them* how to solve problems and achieve their aspirations, so that's a part of her destiny, too.

Whatever your passion is, don't dismiss it just because you think other people might consider it uninteresting or unimportant. If you feel most alive and joyful when you're walking your dog or planting vegetables in your garden, reflect on what it is about those experiences that so inspire and engage you. It may very well lead you to discover what your destiny is.

When you're in your bliss and achieving your life purpose, your emotions are in balance. So, if you'd like to return to that state and align yourself with your destiny, you can choose to bring yourself back into emotional harmony.

Balancing Your Emotions to Achieve Your Destiny

I love to watch athletes in competition and see how their confidence, determination, and competitive spirit drive them to do their best and be number one. Yet the very emotions that allow them to be great at sports may not be the ones that are best suited for their personal life. Imagine a top athlete at home saying to his wife, "Sorry, but I can't take you to the 7:15 movie like I promised, since I'm cleaning the stove, and I just realized the oven needs scrubbing, too. I'm determined to get this kitchen absolutely spotless. There's no stopping me—I know I can make it perfect!"

There's a time for fierce determination and confidence and a time to tone down those emotions and turn up the volume on feelings such as kindness and love. The feelings that are most useful at work may be different from the ones that are most beneficial in your family life or in your friendships.

I'm not saying that if you're an athlete, you need to compartmentalize your emotions, checking your determination and confidence at the door when you get home or letting go of any kindness, empathy, or love upon entering the sports arena. In fact, all these emotions are useful in any circumstance. An athlete might be determined to improve his communication with his wife and feel confident that he can do it and that this will benefit his marriage. At the same time, although he may be a fierce competitor, he can be a good sportsman because he feels kindness toward his opponents, even when he's intent on winning. The point is that in different situations, a different set of dominant emotions is required.

So if you recognize that you need to make an emotional switch, how do you shift from moderate joy to all-out elation, from anger to mere irritation, from agitation to calm, or from insensitivity to kindness? To start, you have to recognize the connection between emotions, thoughts, and behaviors.

Emotions, Thoughts, and Behaviors

Thoughts, feelings, and behaviors all influence each other, but the strongest force is our emotions—and that's why it's so important to take control of, and balance, them. While we may act or think obsessively, we only do so when our behavior or thoughts are driven by strong emotions. For instance, if people are addicted to alcohol, they reach for that glass of wine or vodka again and again because when they drink, they stimulate the pleasure centers in their brain and experience a false sensation of joy, well-being, calm, or confidence. While alcoholics may be determined not to drink and to never think about doing so—and might even clear out their liquor cabinet so that they can't pour themselves a stiff one—their strong desire to feel the emotions that drinking creates for them may overrule their attempts to control their thoughts and behaviors.

In the same way, if we obsessively think about something, it's because strong emotions are driving our thoughts. When we're facing a challenge and we're trying to think through our options, if our feelings aren't overwhelming us, we can readily become distracted, finding it easy to pull our attention away from the subject for a while. Thoughts such as *I wonder what would happen if I approached the situation from this perspective?* might pop up while we're in the shower or walking through the grocery store, and we'll go into a creative mode as we think, but we don't get upset or obsessive. However, when a strong emotion is driving our thoughts, it's much harder to shake them. Suddenly, we have insomnia as we spend the early-morning hours fearfully reflecting on what might happen to us, or we endlessly reminisce about a former romantic partner because we're caught up in grief. It's our emotions that trap us in obsessive thoughts.

All Emotions Are Available to You

To achieve your destiny, you have to be able to feel certain positive emotions at a high level. You might think that you don't have the capacity to experience particular emotions, but I can assure you that you do. Inside you lies a multitude of emotions—you just have to access them, and there are several ways to do so.

Experiencing Emotions Through Art

We all get in touch with a wide range of emotions, switching between them very dramatically when we watch gripping movies, read books that move us, or experience any art form that speaks to our core. Recently I was at a conference that featured speeches and workshops given by many celebrities, from Lance Armstrong to Bill Clinton. One of the performers set to entertain the audience was Toronto singer/songwriter Amy Sky. While she wasn't the star of the conference, she might as well have been, because she seemed to be performing as if she were in front of a stadium full of rabidly enthusiastic fans. She exhibited joy and playfulness; and as I watched her, I found myself connecting with my own feelings of passion, enthusiasm, and humor.

Although I'm not a singer or performer, Amy was able to stir emotions in me that I could use in my own work and life. She did so by immersing herself in these feelings. Had she stopped to think, *Oh, these people don't really want to see me* or *This is just a money gig; I'll save the real performance for the next time I'm in front of my fans,* she wouldn't have had the effect on me that she did. If we open ourselves up to the positive emotions expressed through art, we can create them in ourselves.

Experiencing Emotions Through Interactions with Others

As the old sayings go, "Misery loves company" and "Laughter is infectious." The people we surround ourselves with can affect our emotions, and vice versa. When cyclist Lance Armstrong was facing a dire diagnosis of cancer, he knew that he had to find a physician who believed in his ability to be healed. To fight such a challenging battle, he felt that he needed to draw upon the faith and determination of his doctor, as well as his own.

It's good to be aware of whether the people you spend time with help you lift your mood or make it more difficult for you to stay positive—in other words, choose your companions carefully. Spending a large amount of time around those who always see the negative side of life and tell you about every depressing story they heard on the news may not just affect you in the moment . . . it may impact you overall. You'll start to feel your energy dragging and your mind creating thoughts such as *What's the point?* and *I'm fooling myself. There's no way I can do this.* If you don't consciously work at balancing your emotions around such people, your joyfulness, creativity, determination, and other positive emotions will diminish; and your feelings of hopelessness and melancholy will increase.

Then, too, when you're around people who are gossipy and unkind, you're likely to find yourself giving in to more judgmental, smug, and even cruel emotions. Even participating in mean-spirited gossip about celebrities isn't harmless. It can increase your feelings of unkindness and decrease those of sympathy—and that may carry over to how you feel about, and treat, the people in your life.

On the other hand, making a deliberate decision to spend more time around those who do help you feel positive can make a big difference in your mood. If you're surrounded by individuals who lack compassion and empathy, but *you* want to feel compassionate and empathetic more often and more intensely, seek out people who experience those emotions regularly. One of my clients has a friend who's very playful and creative, and she makes a point to have a "girls' night out" with this person regularly. By eating dinner with her and having fun trying new activities (such as karaoke), she connects to her own playfulness and creativity.

Experiencing Emotions Through Memory and Imagination

If you want to feel an emotion, you can also access it through memory or imagination. Let's say that you're in a job that you find uninspiring, and you'd love to make a change but haven't a clue what else you could do for a living. You know that feeling inspired will help you discover and explore all the options available to you, but you're stuck feeling melancholy. You can't even remember the last time you felt enthusiastic about work or had any fresh ideas about what job you might enjoy—yet I'm sure that at some point in your life, even for a brief moment, you knew what it was like to feel inspired.

Maybe as a child you were enthusiastic about a job that you felt certain you could have when you grew up. I know someone who loved caring for his pet turtles so much that when he was eight years old, he decided to become a turtle farmer someday. Inspired by his hobby, he wrote to his state's department of agriculture and asked for information on turtle-farming opportunities there. I can just imagine the amusement of some bored local official upon reading this enthusiastic letter from a little boy and having to break the news to him that alas, he couldn't help him with his occupational goal! Yet this boy's enthusiasm for doing something he loved drew him to find his calling as an adult in a career that still connected him with inspiration: He became a minister and revitalized the church he was assigned to with his creative revision of the traditional service. If you can connect to a positive feeling that you remember experiencing, you can re-create it.

What were you inspired to do as a child that later you convinced yourself was silly or stupid? Did you color the sun green when you drew a picture, only to have the teacher tell you that it was the "wrong" shade for the sun? Were you inspired to travel when you were a teenager, only to be told that your plans were "impractical"? If you close your eyes and get past the skeptic in your head that has squelched many of your ideas over the years, I'll bet that you can conjure up a time when you were inspired.

You can use your memory to connect to any positive emotion you'd like to feel. In your childhood, you experienced a range of emotions. You hadn't yet developed the skill of repressing them when someone thought that they were inconvenient. What's more, you created emotions all the time when you were playing.

Remember when you were very young and played with your friends? Everything seemed so real because in your imagination, you made it that way. Your dolls or action figures didn't just have names; they had personalities, feelings, and powers. When you got older, though, your toys didn't hold the magic that they once did. You stopped being as imaginative as you were in the past, and you forgot how to pretend—which is a very important skill.

When I was about 12 years old, I remember that my favorite place in the world was in an area behind a school near my house. There was a small stream that flowed through a large metal tube, creating a small waterfall. To me, that flowing water was exquisitely beautiful and peaceful, so I'd go there alone and imagine that my life was equally calm and lovely. By pretending that everything was wonderful, I was able to feel contentment, safety, and happiness . . . I actually created those feelings.

Now, I also remember playing with my sister on top of two small canoes, one red and one yellow, at the lake where we had a summer cottage. We'd climb up on them as they floated in the water, then carefully balance our feet on their edges and pretend that the lake was an ocean. We'd get frightened and excited at the same time, seeing how much we could rock them before tipping them over and splashing into the cold water. I didn't realize it then, but we were playing at managing our emotions, feeling the fear that comes with taking risks but not letting it stop us from having fun.

If you're afraid of risk and have trouble feeling confidence and faith in the unknown, see if you can't access a memory of having done so and experienced positive results. In a sense, what I'm suggesting is that you become like an actor, imagining that you're going through the emotions that you want to feel and creating them with your mind. Jodie Foster once said that her advice to a child actor she was directing was to "pretend really, really well." You, too, need to pretend really, really well.

A great way to accomplish this is to close your eyes and visualize yourself in the experience you'd like to have. You don't need to narrate your vision or think in words. Just see yourself in the situation you'd like to experience. It's even better if you have access to places or objects that will help you imagine what it's like to be onstage, to live in the country, or to own a home. . . . I did so and ended up with the house of my dreams.

Pretending to Have the House I Loved

Many years ago when my ex-husband, Charles, and I decided to divorce, we listed our house for sale. At the time, it was a downward market and homes weren't being bought. Ours was also located outside the city, and country homes typically were even more difficult to sell. However, it was very important to me that we sell that house with all its memories so that I could buy a new one for Michel and me.

Patiently, I waited for a buyer. While the house was listed, I began a search for my new home, attending open houses and visiting new-home showrooms. Charles would ask me, "Peggy, why are you bothering to go and look at houses? You have no money to buy one!" He was absolutely right: Because the real-estate market was declining, we were losing equity in our home every day. It was listed for less than what we paid for it, and we'd lowered the price twice since it went up for sale.

But I was dead set on my goal: I would own a home. And not just any home—I clearly described it and wrote it on a Goal Card that I carried with me, stating: "I, Peggy McColl, am enjoying living in my gorgeous four-bedroom house, which is beautifully decorated and fully furnished, has a two-car garage, and is in a modern subdivision on a nice lot, in a neighborhood with lots of bike trails and parks for Michel and me to enjoy." My son was two and a half at the time, and I felt that it was important for us to have a nice home in an area where there were other small children he could play with and where we could have access to nature.

One day I heard about an interesting raffle in our city. It was called the "Dream of a Lifetime" contest, and for a $100 ticket, you could have a chance to win the grand prize of a large four-bedroom home that was completely furnished and professionally decorated and land-scaped. The Dream Home, as the contest called it, came complete with two new cars in the garage; a year's worth of groceries; and all legal costs, moving expenses, and cleaning services for one year totally paid for. I thought, *Perfect!* This was a great solution to my situation. I simply had to win that house.

The Dream Home was open to visitors during the day, so I drove out to it, passing several parks and bike trails along the way. These were good signs! When I arrived, I noticed that the house had three bathrooms, a yard, and a two-car garage; and it was located in a nice, modern subdivision.

I walked in the front door and immediately fell in love with the house. I started to picture living there. I sat in all the rooms and visual-ized. There was a woman house-sitting the Dream Home, and she let me take my time wandering through it. I sat with her at the kitchen table, imagining that this was my home and she'd come to visit me. I gazed out the window at the newly fallen snow in the backyard and thought, *This is what it will be like at Christmastime when we live here.*

Upstairs, I went through all of the rooms. I decided which one would be Michel's. I lay on the large bed in the master bedroom and imagined myself sleeping on it. I climbed into the big, two-person tub, picturing what it would be like to have a wonderful warm bubble bath in it. As I sat there, I imagined the smell of the bath oil and the feel of the warm water against my skin. I kept my clothes on, of course, but the effect was the same as if I were actually luxuriating in my bath. I felt tranquil as I relaxed in the tub and got in touch with a sense of joy and even bliss.

I came back to visit the house several times, and on each occasion, I walked around inside of it, visualizing myself living there with Michel.

In fact, the house remained open right up until the day of the drawing, so I'd stop by there, imagining that I was driving home from work, and then I'd go for walks around the neighborhood. I also changed my Goal Card, adding the address of the home to the description that I'd already written. Finally, on December 7, the Dream of a Lifetime drawing was held.

A local doctor won the house.

What did I do? . . . I changed my Goal Card, simply removing the address. I didn't lose sight of my dream.

Several months passed. Our house still hadn't sold. I asked Charles if he'd be willing to keep the house if I left and took no money from him for it and none of the furniture. He agreed. We determined an appropriate shared-custody schedule for Michel and set a date for when we'd part ways as husband and wife.

I decided to take a drive past the Dream of a Lifetime home. It had been four months since the doctor had won it. As I drove down the street, I saw that the Dream Home had a For Sale sign on the lawn—I figured it was a "sign" for me. I called the real-estate agent and said, "I want to make an offer on this house."

Within 30 minutes, the agent arrived. We sat at the dining-room table (all of the furniture was still there), and she told me that the doctor was selling the house and didn't need any of the furniture. I wrote up an offer that would allow me to move into the home and occupy it for a period of time and close at a later date. This idea just came to me. When I'd called the agent, I had no idea how I'd pay for it, but I knew that I'd find a way (at that time, you didn't need preapproval for a loan to make an offer on a home). When we're committed, there's always a way.

Two months later, Michel and I moved into our new home. We loved it! It was absolutely perfect. However, I wasn't the owner yet; I was an "occupant," with an agreement to purchase and a firm closing date. Now I had to come up with the money. Honestly, I knew in my heart that I would do it, but I wasn't sure how.

Interestingly enough, I worked for a company that was about to go public with its stock. The IPO (initial public offering) was set. I'd saved some money for the close of my house and put every dollar into shares of stock. The IPO was fixed for October, and my house was set to close on December 1. Then the date of the IPO was moved to November 26. All of the money that I'd raised was now tied up in stock, and I had no idea which direction it would move. If it went down and I didn't have the money for the closing, I'd have to pack up and move out right away.

Was I nervous? You bet, but I refused to give up. I maintained a feeling of certainty and removed any negative thoughts when they entered my mind. I had clearly defined my goal, and I was focused like a laser on making it happen. I developed an unwavering faith.

On November 26, the company went public, and the stock shot up like a rocket. I sold the shares immediately, and on December 1, I closed the deal on my home: I owned the Dream of a Lifetime home, and I lived there with my son for eight more years before selling it for a very healthy profit and buying another house.

Now I could have gotten a dream home another way. I could have changed my thoughts and figured out exactly how to make more money in order to buy the right property when it came along. I could have altered my behavior, working longer hours to make enough money to ensure that I could buy one. Instead, I used the power of my emotions, balancing the fear and uncertainty with heavy doses of joy, confidence, and calm. When I was in the Dream of a Lifetime home, pretending to be its owner, I created feelings of well-being and certainty. In actually experiencing these emotions, I manifested what I desired and brought the house to me. Of course, it didn't come to me exactly as I'd planned, but it *did* come to me, as a result of my balancing my emotions.

My point isn't that you should rush out and commit yourself to buying a home without checking into financing. I happen to be someone with a high tolerance for risk; and in this case, I had unshakable confidence that I would come up with the money for the home. What I want you to realize is that you, too, can manifest what you desire by connecting with your emotions, because they're extremely powerful forces.

In the next chapter, we'll look at the nature of your emotions, because the more you know about them, the easier it will be to carefully select the ones that you want to experience and use to attract the life of your dreams.

❦❦❦

CHAPTER TWO

The Nature and Value of Your Emotions

Emotions seem very real because we experience them physically and perceive them through our senses. Everywhere in the world, and even in the animal kingdom, the outward expressions of certain emotions are very similar. We can witness when a dog or an ape is angry, baring its teeth, or when a person tightens his jaw muscles in rage. When we ourselves are upset or afraid, our blood pressure and heart rate increase and we feel the pounding in our veins. When animals or humans are surprised, we see their eyes open wider and their pupils dilate. Charles Darwin theorized that there must be some sort of physiological, genetic component to emotions that we share with other creatures who—although they may have a shorter range of emotions than we do—also experience fear, sadness, and anger.

The Physicality of Emotions

Recently neuroscientist Dr. Candace Pert discovered evidence of the physical nature of emotions. Her research has found that emotions are neuropeptides—strings of amino acids (or proteins) that swim through the liquid surrounding our cells until they hook up with receptor sites that will receive them on cell walls. Once they stick to these sites, the neuropeptides download information that affects the functioning, reproduction, and health of the cell. Dr. Pert says that this phenomenon would explain the mind-body connection and how we can actually make ourselves sick or healthy through experiencing emotions such as fear, anger, or bliss. Downloading rage, for instance, might make a cell divide too quickly, causing duplication errors and creating precancerous and cancerous cells. While much of this is still theory, it's interesting to think about how our emotions might affect us on a cellular level.

Like all people, you experience emotions physically. In fact, when you've felt a strong emotion, before you could even identify it, you might have been aware of how your body felt—tense or relaxed, energized or weary. Once you noticed your shallower breathing or your tightened neck muscles and thought about what you were experiencing, you were able to label your emotion.

Every day, you guess at what other people are experiencing emotionally by observing their facial expressions, body language, breathing, and vocal changes. You might have taken offense once at an e-mail or instant message that seemed curt, sarcastic, or unkind because you had no physical cues to help you figure out whether the sender was angry or irritated with you, and the writer didn't use an emoticon such as :-) or an abbreviation such as LOL (laughing out loud) to indicate that he or she was kidding. Some children don't have the ability to read facial expressions, tone of voice, or body language; and unless they're trained in how to decode this physical evidence of emotion, they take words at face value, missing the nuances of communication that the rest of us take for granted. Think of phony smiles that show muscle tension or eyes filled with tears that clue us in to how someone is feeling even when a person's words give us a different message.

People who are very good at perceiving emotions are picking up on many subtle physical cues. A top female poker player pays attention to her opponent's breathing and the size of his or her pupils to determine whether the person is lying. A lie detector can identify changes in heart rate so subtle that liars don't realize that they're showing physical evidence of discomfort with their false statements.

Our language reflects our awareness that emotions seem to be bodily experiences. If we're sad or disappointed, we say we're experiencing "heartache." If we're certain of something, we declare: "I feel it in my bones."

But just as our emotions can chemically affect our cells, the chemicals in our body can impact our emotions.

Chemical Influences on Emotions

The theory that neuropeptides are emotions started with the discovery of receptors on the surface of cells that allow the neuropeptides to stick to them and transfer information. This was a crucial breakthrough for pharmacologists because it meant that we finally validated the theory of how drugs work in the body: They adhere to these receptor sites and download information that tells the cell what it needs to do.

When we laugh, our bodies create hormones called endorphins, which make their way to our cells' receptor sites—but those very same sites may respond to artificial endorphins that are created in a laboratory. This explains why mood-altering drugs such as morphine and Prozac can affect us. The chemicals in these drugs actually change our emotions.

Even if you aren't deliberately trying to influence your body and your mood with prescription drugs, you might be manufacturing your own biochemicals that are impacting your emotional state. During some parts of their menstrual cycle, many women experience hormonal changes that make them more sensitive or irritable than they are at other times. Certain foods can affect mood, too. A number of women feel more relaxed after they've eaten chocolate, while some children become overly excited after ingesting certain food dyes or additives. And strange as it might seem, even sunlight can affect our mood: Absorbing it allows us to create serotonin, a feel-good hormone that we need to manufacture to avoid depression. Some people suffer from seasonal affective disorder, becoming very sad and pessimistic due to a lack of sunlight and serotonin. Full-spectrum lighting can improve their moods dramatically.

It's important to recognize just how strongly chemicals can influence our emotions. A woman I know who'd never experienced PMS was surprised that after giving birth, she felt a profound sense of sadness and loneliness. Holding her baby, she wept, and even as she did so, her mind clicked in and said, *Wait a minute—I bet this is that postpartum depression that the nurse warned me about!* She remembered learning that after labor the mix of hormones in a woman's body is changed drastically, and this can cause depression. Even as she thought about this and was intrigued, she still felt sad and lonely for several hours, despite her efforts to talk herself out of such feelings. However, she realized that these were emotions that would fade once her body's chemistry came back into balance.

The Energy of Emotions

Emotions have energy, and just as the sound waves created by a tuba and a piccolo are different, so too is the energetic vibration of each emotion. If you're experiencing joy, you're sending out a vibration of joy, and the universe will respond by bringing you more of it. If you're experiencing discouragement, you're emitting a vibration of discouragement, and you'll draw to yourself pessimistic people and disheartening events. This is why it's very important to experience positive emotions: Like a magnet, you can actually draw to you situations and individuals that will match the emotion you create. You have the ability to attract the life of your dreams by experiencing feelings that pull in circumstances, people, and opportunities that match up with your positive mood.

Creating a vibration of abundance—a feeling that you're wealthy and have all that you need—will actually *create* abundance. If you think, *I'd like to have more money,* you're admitting to the universe that you're short on wealth, and you're generating a feeling of lack instead of prosperity. If you state an affirmation about what you think is going to happen, such as "The right romantic partner is on the way to me," again, you're creating a sense of lack—in this case, that of romantic love and companionship in the present. To get what you want, you have to feel that you have it already. You might imagine yourself sharing a laugh with your partner, and experience what that feels like. Or you could create an affirmation such as "I have romance and companionship in abundance" and repeat it regularly to create the feeling and vibration of abundance. It's *not* enough to simply say the words. You really must experience the emotion of the affirmation in order for it to have powerful effects on your life.

As you engage in positive emotions more often, you may find that people who aren't vibrating emotions that match yours are still drawn to you. This is because they pick up on the fact that you're joyful, confident, inspired, and so on, and they want to feel those things, too. However, you won't be attracted to *them* because they don't match your energy. You can continue experiencing your strong, positive emotions and hope that they'll choose to match the vibration of your feelings and become joyful, confident, and inspired themselves.

They may respond favorably, or they may block themselves from the positive emotions they're attracted to, turning away from you rather than changing their outlook. If clients say to me, "Peggy, I want to be confident like you, instead of worried and fearful about success," I'll work with them on creating confidence, but if they truly aren't ready to feel that emotion, they'll drift away. They choose not to match my vibration, and our partnership naturally ends.

The Reality and Unreality of Emotions

Now that I've explained the very real, very physical aspects of emotions, I have to tell you that ultimately, emotions aren't real at all . . . they're illusions.

Of course, emotions *feel* real, just as the chair you're sitting on feels real, along with the sound of the traffic or the birds outside your window. The material world seems very real, and we believe what our senses tell us about it.

However, the chair that you're sitting on isn't actually solid at all; rather, it's a buzzing mass of energy. It's made up of waves of light and tiny particles that seem to be pieces of matter, but behave like energy or light . . . so you're actually sitting on a buzzing cloud. Everything solid around you is likewise a buzzing cloud—and indeed, even *you* are made up of light energy. The sounds coming into your ears and being interpreted by your brain as honking geese or car horns are actually vibrational waves of energy. So as real and tangible as the material world seems, the reality is that it's made up of energy and light.

Think for a moment about light. You know that it's clear and brilliant—without any color—but the moment that you break it up, it's split into different hues. You can see this effect when you place a crystal prism on a shelf by a sunny window. The shades of the rainbow will appear on your walls, as the sunlight is broken into rays of red, orange, yellow, green, and so on. The color green is still light, but it has its own vibrational energy, which is a little different from that of yellow or blue. The green flickering on the wall appears to be real because your eyes can perceive it, but when it's immersed in the light coming through the window, unbroken by a prism, you don't observe it. All you see is the light; the green has ceased to be.

Emotions work in the same way: They're rays of energy, broken off from the illumination that exists within us. At our core, who we really are is pure light, pure love. We contain all our emotions, yet they all dissolve in the brilliance of such love.

When we're connected to Spirit, in a state of complete communion with divine caring, emotions don't exist. We don't enter into this world feeling worried, angry, or resentful. We don't even experience positive feelings when we come out of the womb. We only know one emotion, and that's love, because Spirit *is* love.

Just as white light contains every color, within Spirit, all the emotions are immersed in one gargantuan emotion—love. Engulfed by it, the unique qualities of each individual feeling dissolve.

So when we're connected to Spirit, deep in meditation and experiencing a much higher level of awareness, the emotions that feel so real and so very important to us when we're in everyday consciousness no longer exist . . . they're absorbed into light. And dark emotions, such as fear and sadness, disappear in the brilliant radiance of love.

Choosing to Let Love Dissolve Your Emotions

The reason it's important to recognize love's power to absorb and dissolve other emotions is because as potent as they can be, ultimately, each of them is an illusion—and a short-lived one at that (unless we harbor them and continually re-create the experience of them). We foster our emotions with our behaviors and thoughts, and that extends their lifetime. Knowing this, we can choose to manifest them, or we can opt to feel love and dissolve them.

Let's say that you're feeling jealous of a neighbor who seems to possess everything that you don't right now. Rather than focusing on what you have that she doesn't (and coming to the conclusion that we all have our challenges and our gifts), you direct your thoughts toward validating your feeling of jealousy, enlarging and enhancing it. You notice that she has a bigger house and a more toned body, and you tell yourself that she leads a carefree, "charmed" life. You convince yourself that "everything" comes easily for her, while "nothing" does for you. You engage in distorted thinking in order to feel justified in your envy, and you dismiss any evidence that your rival isn't better off than you are. You complain to a friend of yours, "I can't stand her. Her life is so perfect," and your friend says, "Didn't you hear? She's been diagnosed with breast cancer."

Instantly, your feelings change: Your jealousy and unkindness vanish—replaced by guilt, empathy, and even fear, because you start thinking about how fragile your own life is. Then, when you access the well of your compassion, any sense of guilt or fear disappears. You experience only love for your neighbor.

Knowing that emotions are temporary and can be absorbed by love, you can put them into perspective and use them as tools to achieve your destiny. If a feeling is serving you, then you'll want to maintain or even enhance it. If it's hurting you, you'll want to let go of it, learning from it if you can. Whatever your choice is, recognize that even the strongest of emotions—such as deep grief—will eventually fade. They're a natural part of the human experience, but they're absorbed by the light of Spirit.

If you've experienced a great loss recently, you may have trouble believing that you'll ever find comfort. However, knowing that you're not alone in your suffering and that life goes on even when you feel crippled by sorrow can help you slowly switch out of grief and move forward, embracing life again.

There's a Buddhist teaching tale about a woman who came to the Buddha because she'd lost her child. She was devastated by grief and asked him to revive her baby. The Buddha said to her, "If I am to bring your child back to life, you must visit every house in the village and bring me a mustard seed from each one that has not experienced death." The woman thanked him and went off to gather mustard seeds from her neighbors so that the Buddha would give life to her child once again. But every time she visited a home, the residents would tell her of a death they'd experienced; therefore, she didn't take a mustard seed from them. This went on for a year, with the woman knocking on door after door, seeking a house that had been untouched by death. Finally, she realized what the Buddha had been trying to teach her: Death and sorrow are a part of the human experience, and we have to accept that. However, we don't have to remain in a state of grief if we choose to experience positive feelings instead.

To Feel Good Is to Feel God

I once heard that to feel good is to feel God, and I believe that this is true. Choose to feel good and you'll be feeling God. Decide to experience love and you'll be linked to the divine source. Ask yourself, *Is this emotion helping me feel good, and connected to Spirit?* If the answer is no, you've taken a wrong turn, moving away from your destiny.

One way to stay on the course of your destiny is to follow the advice of Neale Donald Walsch. In his book *Friendship with God,* he suggests that we ask one thing: *"What would love do now?"* Posing this question to yourself each morning and answering it will guide you how to live your life in the face of all the opportunities and challenges that will present themselves each day.

You can also make an effort to uplift yourself and experience God by deliberately choosing to engage in activities that will make you feel good, even when you're tempted to wallow in your current state. Whether or not you're justified in being sad because you're without a romantic partner and haven't had one for a long time, or in feeling hurt because someone said something cruel to you, isn't the point. You may be justified in experiencing any number of painful emotions, but that doesn't mean you have to *choose* to feel them.

I'm sure there have been times in your life when you reluctantly dragged yourself to a party even though you were in no mood to celebrate, only to feel your emotions shift once you got there. Similarly, you might have been in a dark and pessimistic mood, but when your child walked in with a smile on her face, enthusiastically babbling about something, you chose to connect with her positive feelings and let your negative ones dissolve. Sometimes just getting up and taking a walk outside in the sunshine can help you switch out of melancholy and into inspiration, or out of sadness and into happiness.

While you can't always shift your emotions as quickly and easily as you'd like to, if you're able to accept that they're temporary experiences in the material world and you can shorten their life span, it will be easier for you to continue trying to achieve balance.

Becoming Aware of Your Emotions

When you're experiencing a strong emotion, your physical response may be so intense that you immediately start thinking about what's happening, trying to explain it to yourself. However, sometimes you aren't able to recognize your emotions and label them, for whatever reason. In some cases, the problem is that your physical experience of an emotion is so subtle that you don't recognize that you're feeling anything at all.

Let's say that you've just run into a neighbor at the grocery store. You chat for a few moments and realize that you're feeling vaguely uneasy or upset, but you carry on the conversation with no tension in your voice and no clear sign that your negative emotion is affecting you. Very quickly your mind dismisses the idea that you're uncomfortable, because the dialogue is continuing and someone is asking you to move your cart so that she can get around you. You say good-bye to your neighbor, focus on finishing your shopping and checking out, pack your groceries into the car, start driving, and then stop at a red light. As you're sitting there, the feeling of uneasiness comes up again. This time, even though you don't feel your jaw muscles tightening, your hands shaking, or any other obvious sign of a strong emotion, the distractions are gone and you're more aware that something is happening inside you.

In the quiet, you're able to tune in to what you're feeling. Maybe your stomach doesn't feel quite right. Perhaps your teeth are slightly clenched. In your mind, you can ask yourself, *What's going on here? What am I feeling, and why?*

Because your emotions can emerge so quickly and unexpectedly, you can become distracted by everything you have to do and push them aside. It's often inconvenient to tune in to your feelings. After all, you have groceries to buy and unpack, phone calls to make, and a million things on your to-do list. But if you're going to achieve your destiny and feel joy and contentment, you have to develop the habit of slowing down to observe your emotions.

Suppressing Emotions

Another reason you might quickly dismiss an emotion is that somewhere along the way when you were growing up, you got the message that it's not okay to experience that feeling. You learned to squelch it quickly and find something to occupy your mind so that you wouldn't think about it.

Many people, especially women, have been taught that they shouldn't feel anger or competitiveness. Men are often told that they shouldn't feel vulnerable. Sometimes kids get the clear message that they ought to hide their confidence because people might think that they're stuck-up. Other children are taught that being calm and quiet is "boring." They learn that emotional turmoil is a good thing, and when they grow up, they're so used to being caught up in these dramas that they don't realize how wonderful it is to experience tranquility.

Whatever it is that's convinced you to suppress what you're feeling, if you have this habit, it's vitally important that you break it. As you'll learn in later chapters of this book, all emotions—even the destructive ones—can be useful tools in helping you achieve your destiny, so you need to experience them.

When you make a point of noticing your subtle sense of unease or unhappiness, you take the first step toward uncovering what you're feeling and making a conscious decision about whether or not you want to let go of that emotion, increase it, or learn from it before dissolving it in the light of love. When you're stopped at a red light or experiencing a quiet moment, ask yourself, *What's going on here? Why am I upset?*

One reason you might not know the answer is that to your conscious mind there was no reason for you to be unsettled. However, your subconscious mind made a judgment of the situation so quickly that your body instantly created the feeling of discomfort. Letting yourself become curious will allow you to discover what that emotion is telling you.

Emotions as Indicators

When you feel uneasy and don't know why, without judging yourself as foolish and dismissing your perception, you can simply ask, *Why would I be feeling uneasy right now?* The answer might be that deep inside you sense that you're unworthy. Since you've just experienced something that your subconscious mind decided was evidence of that fact, you began to *feel* unworthy.

I used to be very sensitive to criticism because I had low self-esteem. Even if my husband had no intention of criticizing me, I was prone to interpreting what he said as a sign of disapproval. I thought that I was reacting to his words, but what I was actually responding to was my own thought process.

When I was growing up, I didn't feel as though I got enough praise from my parents. What's more, when they were upset or frustrated, they would say things to me such as "What's the matter with you? Can't you do anything right? You're useless!" I'm sure that to them, these words didn't mean much. They were simply irritated and expressing it. Like many people of their generation, they didn't know what a strong, detrimental effect such statements can have on a child. Kids, like adults, will often latch onto something negative and dwell on it, forgetting the positive things that have been said.

I internalized the message that I was useless and unworthy. Then, when I was grown up, I'd seize upon any evidence that this was the case and immediately re-create those feelings from my childhood. Of course, I had no idea that I was doing this—I thought that I was feeling unworthy because of something someone said or did to me. I didn't realize that I could choose to recognize my habit of buying into the old beliefs about myself and reject them. I didn't understand that I could decide not to feel useless. Over time, I learned that instead of judging my husband, his comments, or myself, I could replace judgment with curiosity and wonder. I could stop and think, *Isn't it interesting that I responded in that way? What's that about?*

Choosing to Examine What Your Emotions Reveal

When you feel uncomfortable, it's only natural to resist this process of exploring your emotions. If you're ill at ease, irritated, or blue rather than completely stressed out, furious, or depressed, you're more likely to dismiss your mildly unpleasant feeling for fear that looking at it more closely will just make you feel worse. You lose the opportunity to discover the thought patterns that lead you to experience negativity. You miss the chance to consciously decide not to engage in the thinking that's stirring up your emotions. It's as if you walk around with huge bags full of garbage tied to you that are trailing behind as you trudge forward. Examining your unpleasant emotions will help you cut loose those trash bags that contain thoughts such as *I'm not successful, and I'll never make something of myself* or *I'm too needy for anyone to love.*

Exploring your emotions allows you to say, "Oh, I know where this is coming from. When my friend plucked that stray hair off my coat, I was unconsciously thinking that she was judging me for being sloppy. I was upset because as a child I felt that way when my mother would call me a slob and tell me to clean up my room." When you can see the origin of your emotion, you can learn from it and tell yourself, *I don't think that way anymore, and this emotion doesn't feel good.* Then you can begin to contemplate which emotion you'd prefer to experience.

Then, too, when you think that you're being offended by someone, recognize that you might be experiencing anger, guilt, or embarrassment because what they're telling you has some validity and you haven't accepted that truth about yourself. Maybe you *are* sloppy. If so, how do you feel about that? Why do you feel that way? You may be judging yourself very harshly. If you are, stop and again create a feeling of curiosity. Ask yourself, *What are the standards and values that I'm trying to live up to, and do I want to change them?*

Being a working mom, I'm often pressed for time. I'll often make the deliberate decision to spend a few extra moments with my son talking or doing something fun rather than cleaning the house. I'm comfortable with this decision. If I were ambivalent about my choice to let the housekeeping slide a bit, I might become irritable or feel guilty if my mother were to come by to visit me, pick up a sponge, and begin wiping down a counter. Because I'm comfortable with my standards of cleanliness and my choice to trade off a perfectly spotless house for more time with my son, I wouldn't be upset if a visitor felt like cleaning my counters. If I had any emotional reaction, it would be a mild sense of gratitude.

So when you find yourself feeling bad, ask yourself what exactly you're feeling and why, but also be open to the possibility of further exploring the choices you've made so that you can determine if they're working for you. If they are, then you simply need to remind yourself of that fact when you fall back into the habit of judging yourself.

Hidden Emotions

Sometimes your initial emotional experience in a situation conceals what you're really feeling. Out of a sense of self-protection or discomfort, you may subconsciously choose to cover up anger with sadness, ambition with jealousy, and so on.

If you were raised to believe that it's not acceptable to get mad, you might hide your anger by becoming sad in order to distract yourself from your true emotions. However, if you allowed yourself to feel the force of your anger, you might realize just how important it is for you to make changes in your life, and you could make a conscious decision to do so. Unfortunately, most of us are scared of bringing our darkest feelings to the surface. Try to remember that exploring your emotions—getting to the bottom of them and figuring out where they're coming from—will help you make better choices about what thoughts and feelings you'll experience. The short-lived discomfort of confronting a negative emotion that you've been hiding might be worth it in the long run.

For example, if you're feeling down about your relationship, you might talk yourself into staying in it for a long time—for as long as you can tolerate the sadness. However, if the relationship isn't working for you and you can access the strong feeling of anger that's hidden underneath, you could be more inspired to find its roots and start making some changes. You might discover that you need to alter your standards. You could possibly want more out of your relationship—more affection, loyalty, and intimacy—and that's okay. You may not become aware of your need for change if you're simply tolerating your mild sense of sadness that's covering up stronger negative emotions.

The more aware you are of your feelings, the easier it will be to take charge of your destiny and attract the life of your dreams. In the next part of the book, you'll continue to learn about your creative, positive emotions as well as the destructive, negative ones and how you can work with them to create beneficial emotional habits that will help you manifest whatever you desire.

∞∞∞

PART II

YOUR DESTINY SWITCH OF EMOTIONS

CHAPTER THREE

Your Destiny Switch

One of the things I do professionally is act as a Goal-Achieving Mentor for people, helping individuals and companies learn how to attain the results they desire. A while back, I decided that I wanted to find a more effective way to help my clients understand the power of their own emotions—both positive and negative—and their influence on what happens in our lives. I thought about how I might describe the way they work, and one day an image popped into my mind: I envisioned a panel of dimmer switches controlling the emotions, similar to an electrical panel of switches that you might find on a dining-room wall. (The cover illustration depicts a conventional flip switch for the sake of simplicity.) I made a trip to the hardware store, purchased a four-switch panel, and placed labels above and below each of its switches to represent opposite emotions.

Here's what my switch panel looked like:

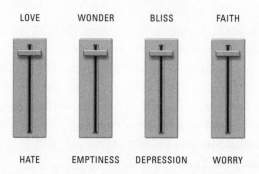

When you pull up any switch on a dimmer-switch panel, you increase the level of light that you're experiencing—or, for our purposes, the degree of positive emotion. If you lower a switch, you become less positive, perhaps even experiencing negative feelings. I call this switch panel of emotions your *Destiny Switch.*

Being the Operator of Your Destiny Switch

All of the emotions on your Destiny Switch are readily available. Accessing them is as easy as entering a dark room and . . . flipping on a switch. Even when you're not feeling the energy of positive, creative emotions, they're inside of you—just as all the colors of the rainbow are contained within a prism. If you choose to experience a certain feeling, you simply have to turn it on.

While it may seem that you're not always in charge of your switches and that other people and events outside of your control can move them down or up, that's not the case. You're the one with your hand on your Destiny Switch. You get to experience the empowerment that comes from recognizing and taking on this awesome responsibility for your emotional well-being. You have the privilege of being in charge of your feelings and your destiny.

I used to think that something outside of me would fix my life and make me feel better, but as long as I held on to that false belief, I remained stuck in an unbalanced, unharmonious place—a dark, unhappy, lonely state. So if I was in a relationship and things weren't going well, I'd expect my partner to say something to make me feel better, which would set him up for failure.

Assuming that someone else can change the way you feel is destructive to any relationship. As Neale Donald Walsch says, having expectations in relationships is a great "love-ender." Now, I'm not saying that you can't have *any* expectations, but you do have to accept that people have flaws and that no one is responsible for your feelings —ever. It's important to have perspective and not to concentrate on the unpleasant behavior of others when you can focus on all their wonderful qualities.

Each of us creates the drama in our relationships, and we can choose *not* to create it. You don't have to make yourself angry because your husband doesn't call to say he'll be late for dinner, or because your daughter leaves her shoes on the floor and you trip over them. If you like, you can simply deal with the situation—pick up the phone or the shoes yourself. Later you can talk to your husband about how it's important to you that he call if he's going to be late, or ask your daughter to try to remember that you don't like clutter on the floor. Alternately, you can choose to not think any further about it because you've decided to work around the particular person's actions.

If you do decide to get upset about someone else's behavior (and this will happen sometimes when you're not feeling a strong sense of love and patience), recognize that you could also choose *not* to get upset. Giving in to anger, resentment, and distrust is always disempowering. You don't have to make such a choice and start to feel as if you're at the mercy of other people and situations that you have no control over. You don't have to undermine your self-confidence and feel less loving toward yourself or others. You can choose to be caring . . . to experience that warm, expansive, uplifting sense that everything is as it should be and we're all connected.

In making this decision, you'll feel love for yourself and everyone around you and raise the volume on your feelings of trust and patience as well. You don't need to create tension and pressure in your relationships—or worse, sabotage them—by choosing to expect others to behave in a certain way. You can feel love no matter how they act. When you do, they'll feel the power of your caring and raise the love lever on their own Destiny Switch.

Today, I know that I'm the one in charge of my destiny and my feelings. I don't need or expect anyone to boost me up. Although it's nice to be told that I'm beautiful and lovable, I don't have to hear it to feel it. I don't need to look to someone else to make me feel good about myself—I choose to feel good regardless. Positive feelings of confidence, self-love, and worthiness flow forth when I decide to raise the lever on any positive emotion. And when I'm comfortable with myself and who I am, I feel blessed and privileged no matter what's happening or how those around me behave.

By not demanding recognition or expecting others to tell you how wonderful you are, you make it easier for them to feel the joy of expressing their appreciation and admiration. You don't weigh them down with the obligation to constantly reassure you. They'll find themselves basking in your positive emotions and inspired to raise the volume on their own joy, patience, and kindness . . . and it will feel natural for them to express those feelings toward you.

On the other hand, if you lower your switches and bring yourself into a negative emotional state, even the most enthusiastic cheerleader won't be able to shift you into a more positive one. All of us filter everything through our belief systems, so when you're feeling bad, you'll dismiss any evidence that contradicts your feelings. Negative emotions can be so powerful that they lead you to talk yourself out of embracing any compliments or encouragement. *You* have to be the one who decides that you've had enough of feeling bad and are ready to make a switch.

The world offers you plenty of opportunities to lower yourself into a negative state—say no to them! And while it's important to infuse yourself with positivity whenever you can by reading upbeat self-help books, reciting affirmations, and so on, keep in mind that these techniques work because you choose to let them. It's you who decides to connect to the confidence and faith that a motivational speaker is communicating . . . he or she isn't doing it for you. It's you who decides to raise the levers of your positive emotions and pull yourself out of negativity.

My fourth epiphany, which I discussed in the Introduction, taught me that you have to be willing to give it all up in order to have it all, and that if you were able to create something once and you lost it, you can create it again. If you've ever experienced joy, confidence, or faith, although you may not be connecting with those emotions at the moment, you can feel them again, no matter what your circumstances are right now. When you suffer a great loss, it's hard to remember that you'll laugh and feel bliss again. It may be more difficult for you to switch to that emotion and keep it at a high level than it would if your situation were different, but you'll be able to do it—I promise. Just as all the colors of the rainbow are in the rays of the sun, all the positive emotions are inside you, waiting to be switched on.

Sometimes it's easy to make the switch to a positive emotion. For instance, good thoughts can lead to your feeling good. I have no problem feeling blissful when I'm lounging on a white-sand beach with the warm sun caressing my skin, listening to the gentle rhythm of the waves. It's a lot more difficult for me to feel joyous when I arrive at the tropical island and learn that my luggage has been lost, there's no shop where I can buy comfortable summer clothes to replace the winter outfit I'm wearing, and my hotel reservation has disappeared somewhere in the computer. But ultimately, I always have the choice to roll up my sleeves and pant legs, relax in a chair, and envision my luggage arriving and my reservation coming up on the computer screen, or to remain open to other positive resolutions.

Raising the level of my faith and calm sends out vibrations that bring situations to me that have a similar vibration, making my luggage and reservation far more likely to appear. I know that I can choose to create a beautiful melody with my vibration, or I can screech out a horrifying sound. I conduct the symphony, and I control my Destiny Switch.

Why You Might Choose to Switch to a Negative Emotion

So why would people choose to lower their positive emotions and pull themselves down into a negative emotional state?

If you were to make this choice, you'd probably do so unconsciously. Your immediate reaction to a situation may be to listen to hidden negative thoughts that pop up automatically, such as *He's being mean to me on purpose, People are always picking on me,* or *I'm such a dummy—of course I'm screwing this up!* You might not realize that thinking in this way will cause you to lower the levels of your positive emotions, bringing you into a negative state. Or you'll instantly envision yourself as a wounded and helpless victim of circumstances and create a feeling of sadness and unworthiness. With these thoughts and images in your head, you unwittingly lower the faith, confidence, and worthiness levers on your Destiny Switch.

The other reason you might choose a negative emotion is that you mistakenly believe that it will make you feel better to indulge in your anger, resentment, or unkindness. Rage seems powerful, and in fact it is—it's like a poison that has the potential to destroy. However, it's important not to choose this emotion because it's just as likely to destroy you as it is whomever you're angry at. Picking anger is like deciding to take poison and expecting the other person to get sick. Then, too, you might convince yourself that you'll feel less hurt and vulnerable—and more powerful—if you're unkind to someone who has been unkind to you. If you indulge in these negative emotions, you can't possibly feel positive . . . instead, you'll experience nothing but negative emotions.

You might also choose negative emotions because you're being affected by PMS, clinical or postpartum depression, or a similar condition that makes it difficult to turn up the volume on positive feelings. There are many treatments that can help you (in addition to the strategies for switching emotions that you'll learn about later in this book), and I encourage you to do your own research and consult with a medical professional.

Even though you'll sometimes be in a negative state temporarily, the good news is that you're always—*always*—in charge of your Destiny Switch. The very moment you recognize that you're feeling bad, you can stop and take a look at what you've just done: You've turned down the volume on a positive emotion. You now have two choices: (1) to decide right now to make a switch; or (2) to continue letting yourself think negatively, feeding a dark emotion and pulling yourself further away from feeling good. You can start thinking about how justified you are in feeling anger, worry, or hopelessness; or you can say to yourself, *This emotion is definitely not making me feel good. It's not helping me, and I'm not going to feel it anymore.* Then, you can ask yourself, *What do I choose to feel right now?* Chances are, the emotion that would best serve you is the opposite of the negative one you're experiencing.

The Scale of Human Emotions

Aristotle was the first to understand the primacy of emotions and how they're paired as opposites. In his book *The Art of Rhetoric,* he matched up anger with calmness, friendship with enmity, fear with confidence, and kindness with unkindness. The Scale of Human Emotions that I've created is based on those pairings I believe to be the most beneficial and empowering—and they're key to achieving your destiny.

You'll notice that each emotion can have several names because every one of us may identify or describe it a little differently from the way another person would. You might feel that you'd like to create your own scale of a particular emotion, but I think that you'll find this one extremely helpful when you're working with your Destiny Switch.

THE SCALE OF HUMAN EMOTIONS	
Love	**Faith**
Adoration/devotion	Belief/assuredness
Like/fondness	Trustfulness
Indifference	Indifference
Dislike	Doubt/disillusionment
Disgust/repulsion	Distrustfulness/cynicism
Hate	**Worry/anxiousness/panic/fear**
Bliss	**Confidence**
Elation	Assuredness
Joy/delight/happiness	Safety
Indifference	Indifference
Melancholy/sadness	Timidity/hesitancy
Misery/despondency	Doubt
Depression	**Insecurity**
Harmony	**Calm**
Unity	Tranquility
Connection	Quietness
Indifference	Indifference
Disconnection	Nervousness/discontent
Disharmony/isolation	Agitation/frustration/irritation
Loneliness	**Rage**
Wonder	**Inspiration**
Curiosity	Enthusiasm
Interest	Stimulation
Indifference	Indifference
Boredom	Listlessness
Distance	Detachment
Emptiness	**Discouragement**

THE SCALE OF HUMAN EMOTIONS	
Kindness	**Abundance**
Carefulness	Comfort/gratitude/expansiveness
Sympathy	Appreciation/well-being
Indifference	Indifference
Insensitivity	Discomfort
Negligence	Want
Unkindness	**Impoverishment**
Worthiness	**Courage**
Grace	Certainty/determination
Esteem	Firmness
Indifference	Indifference
Pity/shame/disgrace	Indecisiveness
Sorrow	Uncertainty
Worthlessness	**Cowardice**

Notice that positive emotions are on the top and negative ones are at the bottom. This is because there's no way to feel a particular positive emotion and its opposite, negative emotion at the same time. If you're experiencing love, adoration, or devotion, hatred isn't in your heart. If you're feeling trust, you have no room for doubt. Of course, the opposite is true as well: If you're in a mood of uncertainty, you can't feel faith unless you move the switch to create that feeling.

The State of Indifference

There are times when you feel as if you're stuck in neutral, unable to move forward or back. Instead of experiencing a positive or a negative emotion, you're in a state of indifference.

It's okay to reach this neutral resting spot and idle for a while as you catch your breath, but you don't want to stay there too long, paralyzed and unable to take the road to your destiny. You may need a boost to help you switch out of indifference.

If you're willing to raise the volume on your positive emotions, you *can* pull yourself out of indifference. However, sometimes it's more motivating to pull a lever downward into negativity for a short time, because the human instinct to move away from pain is even stronger than the drive to move toward pleasure.

A client of mine had recently divorced and felt emotionally numb. The little things she used to take pleasure in did nothing for her mood. She'd try to cheer herself up by spending time with friends, but even if she started laughing and joking and enjoying herself, her happiness dissolved on her way home. It wasn't that she was sad so much as she wasn't feeling anything at all much of the time.

I suggested to her that maybe she was afraid that if she felt any positive emotions, they'd always disappear immediately, and this was making it very difficult for her to feel motivated to raise her levels of positive emotion or maintain her joy, enthusiasm, and inspiration for long. I suggested that she explore her fears and let herself feel sad for a while. You can't talk yourself out of grief, I explained to her, but you can learn from it—and once you do, it's easier to let it go.

In fact, my client decided that it was time for her to face the painful feelings that she'd been avoiding and enter therapy in the hopes of better understanding the huge life change that she'd just experienced. The more she explored her negative feelings, such as anger, sadness, and even unworthiness, the easier it was for her to switch out of them and consciously move up the levers of her calmness, joy, and worthiness. She stopped being stuck in indifference and began creating positive emotions for herself.

The Mix

At any given time, your mix of emotions will be different. You'll have days when you're feeling especially confident, and others when you're feeling more melancholy than usual. When you accept that you're in charge of your Destiny Switch, you'll more clearly see the positions of the levers on your emotions, and you'll know which ones you'd like to adjust.

There's no "right" combination of emotions for everyone at all times. Depending on what you're striving for or the situation that you're in, your own mix may change, and some positive-emotion switches will be in a higher position than others. You can't have every one set on maximum positivity unless you're a master yogi in a state of pure bliss. And if you're at that level of consciousness, you can't deal with checking your mail, driving your child to school, or cooking a meal.

Inevitably, we sometimes choose negative emotions. When I was first immersing myself in self-help literature, I was young and naive enough to think that all the motivational speakers I saw and the authors of self-improvement and inspirational books that I read led blissful lives all the time. I thought that I, too, should be unfailingly positive. When I did experience a negative emotion, I'd feel bad about myself. I didn't realize how unrealistic my expectations of myself were.

You might be inspired, happy, and full of love overall, but of course sometimes you'll feel a niggling sense of self-doubt or a momentary bout of loneliness or sadness. Be kind to yourself when this happens. Remember that as long as you recognize that you're slipping into negativity, you can self-correct by focusing on the emotion that you want to experience and choosing to feel it. Later in this book, I'll provide strategies to help you learn how to do this.

As operator of your Destiny Switch, you can select your mix of emotions. It might be helpful to think of your Destiny Switch as a mixing board used for recorded music. When sound engineers want to hear a little more guitar in the mix, they'll begin raising the lever that controls the volume of that track of music. Or maybe they'd prefer to have the vocals more prominent, so they'll increase the volume on that lever instead. Like a sound engineer, you can choose which emotions you'd most like to feel. You don't really want to try to push every switch up as high as it goes. The nicest mix of music usually features musical dynamics: One instrument will be louder during the verse than during the chorus, while another instrument will be arranged in the opposite way. You might want to focus on a feeling of confidence when you're facing a challenging assignment at work, but center on kindness when you're dealing with a very difficult person who tends to lash out at you. In a later chapter, you'll learn about how and why to focus on four key emotions for achieving any particular goal.

The Invisible String

Even if you're just concentrating on raising the volume of a single positive emotion, it's as if an invisible string connects all the levers on your Destiny Switch so that more than one will move at a time. Create a feeling of faith and you'll soon realize that you're feeling confident, creative, loving, and kind. On the other hand, if you lower one lever in order to encounter a negative emotion, other levers will start to slip downward as well. Allow yourself to experience anger and you'll soon realize that you're also feeling sad, disconnected, and emotionally impoverished.

With such a strong connection between emotions, it's vital that you concentrate on raising the volume on your positive feelings. When you do, you'll be amazed by how much easier it is to avoid slipping into negativity. You'll feel great most of the time, no matter what challenges you face. In the next chapter, you'll learn more about the 12 positive emotions on the Scale of Human Emotions and why they're such powerful tools for creating your destiny.

∞∞∞

CHAPTER FOUR

Choosing Creative Emotions

Listen to a fine symphony and you'll hear harmonious, beautiful music that's more than the sum of its parts. The violins sound exquisite as they sing their melody, and the shimmering cymbals are vibrant as they crescendo with the timpani. The somber but sweet cellos, the playful flutes, and the warm French horn all make lovely music . . . but together, they're even more of a delight.

Positive emotions work collectively like the instruments in a symphony. They harmonize with each other and create the music of life. Nurture any one of them and you'll connect to the endless store of creativity in the universe, raising the volume on other positive feelings as well. It's as if the other emotional instruments can't wait to jump in and create music once you've begun playing even the simplest melody.

You can achieve your destiny by using your creativity and your positive emotions, because feeling any one such emotion will attract events, people, circumstances, and outcomes that resonate to its vibration. Be enthusiastic and enthusiastic people will show up in your life. Experience joy and joyous events will unfold.

How Positive Emotions Attract Positive Circumstances

Every year, I attend a convention for booksellers and buyers called BookExpo America (BEA). I never go with a specific goal in mind, such as *I'll be introduced to six industry movers and shakers and pass out at least 100 business cards.* I simply show up with a positive intention to meet people, talk to them, learn something, and teach them a little about what I do to market books on the Internet. Because I arrive at the convention center filled with enthusiasm, inspiration, joy, and curiosity, I inevitably enjoy a positive experience. The first year I went, I bumped into a friend, and as I began chatting with her, a famous author whom she knew well spotted her and came up to us. When he found out that I didn't know anyone else at the BEA, he offered to take me around and introduce me to people. Because his books are quite popular and he's very well liked, the people I met through him were interested to know who I was, and I made excellent business contacts that benefited me enormously.

A "lucky" event such as this happens when you're filled with positive emotions. Sometimes the ability to attract positive people and opportunities into your life can seem downright magical. You'll go to a dinner party and end up sitting next to someone who has enormous insight into a challenge that you're facing. Or you'll be thinking about how you'd like to work with a certain person you've never met but whom you've heard good things about, and she'll call you out of the blue that very day. This sort of serendipity is no accident: By sending out positive vibrations, you're attracting beneficial people and situations, even when you're not sure exactly who or what might be of help to you.

Whatever you're feeling, you're creating. If you're worried about money matters and experiencing a sense of want, you create a feeling of lack instead of abundance, and your finances worsen. Alternately, if you create a feeling of abundance instead of want, your financial prospects improve.

A friend of mine, Olivia, recently found herself with very little money and many bills after her husband died unexpectedly. Rather than thinking, *Oh no! How will I pay this bill or that bill?* and piling on worry after worry, Olivia chose to stay positive and to pray, saying, "God, I trust that You'll send me what I need." Every day she got in touch with her feelings of faith and abundance . . . and very soon, money began coming in. There was a check from a life-insurance company for a policy her husband had taken out several years previously that Olivia hadn't known about. Her husband's employer also sent her a check she hadn't expected. Even the government mailed her a check, as someone had recently done an audit and it turned out that her husband had been shorted several thousand dollars due to him as disability compensation when he was injured a few years back.

Now Olivia hadn't known that any money was coming, and she didn't have any specific plans for how she could bring more in. However, as soon as she decided to stop stressing out and switch to having faith that the money she needed was on its way to her, it began to arrive. As Olivia learned, positive emotions truly have powerful effects.

In contrast, years ago when I was having financial troubles, I started to dwell on them constantly, thinking about how I could fix my problem. I felt a sense of lack and feared that my money woes would never end. In doing so, I created an even worse situation for myself because I repelled wealth and abundance, and that fed my fear and worry.

Attracting the Life of Your Dreams

Most of us have been told again and again that if we want to live the life of our dreams, we have to work hard for it by setting large goals and breaking them down into manageable "chunks"—small goals that we can push ourselves to achieve on our way to the big ones. This approach may work for some people, but I believe that it keeps us engaged in the same pattern of thinking we always adopt, closing us off to the many ways our goals might be accomplished that we haven't yet figured out (and may never figure out). Frequently I've seen people get what they desire in a form they never would have expected. Certainly, I didn't anticipate that I'd acquire my dream home through a stock sale. By focusing on the emotions of having achieved my goal, I opened myself up to the universe's unpredictable way of making sure that I got what I desired.

I believe in attracting the life of your dreams by thinking big. Connect with what you truly desire, no matter how outlandish, improbable, or impractical it might seem. The universe doesn't recognize the difference between small goals and big ones—it responds to your emotion and intent. If you hope to inhabit your dream home on the lake- or beachfront, you don't have to be practical and envision yourself living in a more modest and affordable house ten miles inland. What you need to be open to is the unusual and unexpected ways in which the universe will grant your wish.

You can't possibly think of all the avenues to achieving your dream. If you connect with the emotions of owning the home or launching the career that you desire, opportunities to bring you closer to that goal will appear, and you'll naturally follow them. You won't have to think about, plan, and agonize over your business card or Website design or struggle with your résumé, because you'll naturally feel the drive to create these items and will make them come into being. You'll do so yourself, or you'll attract someone else who will provide the necessary expertise, perhaps in exchange for some service you can offer.

You never know *how* the life of your dreams will come to fruition, but when you do the work of creating positive emotions, you'll become a magnet, drawing in all that you desire. This is why it's so important to create positive emotions. They can bring you all that you long for without your having to devote enormous amounts of energy to making everything happen.

The Hidden Benefits of Positive Emotions

With so many powerful, enriching, positive emotions available to you as tools for manifesting your dream life, it's important that you don't overlook any of them simply because you have some false ideas about their benefits. You may have grown up in a family or culture that didn't place great value on certain emotions, was dismissive of them, or was even suspicious of their effects. I've worked with female clients who were taught that bravery and determination are masculine qualities, and they had to discard this old, disempowering notion in order to embrace those valuable emotions. Some people have been taught that joy isn't as important as self-sacrifice and being a good person . . . but the happier you are, the more you experience inspiration, abundance, expansiveness, and generosity. You feel compelled to be a better person and help others. Don't underestimate the power and importance of joy!

I've also worked with clients who mistakenly believe that being calm or tranquil isn't as effective as anxiousness and worry. They fear that if they let themselves feel peaceful, they won't be as highly motivated. They're surprised to find that they're more energetic and inspired when they aren't in crisis mode, feeding off of anxiety. Remember that experiencing negative emotions drains you of energy and makes you more discouraged, but a positive feeling fills you with enthusiasm and creativity as you find yourself raising the levels of many other positive emotions all at once.

Faith and confidence are two additional emotions that people sometimes undervalue. They may fear that if they have these feelings, others will think that they're a little crazy or foolish. My ex-husband, Charles, probably thought that I was nuts to check out houses to buy when we were divorcing and I had very little money—but I had plenty of faith that I would end up with the perfect place for my son and me to live. In my work as a Goal-Achieving Mentor, I help people get over their fear of what others might think if they create strong feelings of faith and confidence. Believing that your positive emotional state will attract positive people and events will help motivate you to continue choosing uplifting experiences instead of slipping into negativity.

In fact, fear of what other people might think of you is extremely disempowering. If you feel reluctant to raise the volume on a particular positive emotion, consider whether it's fear that's getting in your way. Ask yourself, *What exactly am I afraid of?* You might be able to learn something about yourself by exploring this question. Determine whether you want to feel that insecurity instead of a powerful, positive emotion. Delve into your fear long enough to figure out where your resistance is coming from, but then let it go.

As you read the following explanations of the 12 key positive emotions—which are based on the Scale of Human Emotions—think about how each of them might help you in your life today, and try to let go of any beliefs you might have that make you resistant to turning up the volume on a particular one. All of these feelings are very beneficial, but the most powerful among them is the emotion that encompasses them all: love.

Love

Love has been described as a bright white light that destroys darkness by causing us to become illuminated from within. When we let the light of our love shine forth, we not only enrich our own lives, but we elevate others' as well. Express caring toward those who are upset or frustrated and you can observe its magical effect as they become inspired to turn up the volume of love on their own Destiny Switch. This emotion makes us feel alive and vibrant, fearless and filled with hope . . . even when darkness surrounds us. The smallest reminder of love encourages us to switch over to it, because we know how fantastic it feels and sense its tremendous power.

One of the reasons why love is such an incredible force is that it multiplies quickly and easily. When you create this feeling in yourself, other people feel inspired to switch into it as well. Their love affects those whom they interact with, and the emotion keeps spreading.

Love can help you overcome any adversity, since it gives you the strength to forgive and to be compassionate. It allows you to witness the good in others and help them see it in themselves. At the same time, it permits you to forgive yourself, too. When you experience love, you're able to carry on despite any obstacles because the emotion fuels you as though it were the most nourishing food in the world. You feel as if you're overflowing with positive energy and kindness.

Love heals and energizes everyone it touches . . . and this world needs healing. That's why it's very important to cherish even those people whom you don't like very much. By raising the level of your love switch, solutions to problems appear because you're open to every positive possibility. Creativity springs forth from the divine source of love within.

Faith

Faith is a belief in things unseen, a conviction that something positive exists even when you don't have tangible evidence for it. There are many different kinds, including faith in God, in the positive outcome of a situation, or in a larger plan for your life that makes sense of the difficulties you've had to suffer. You can have faith in yourself (which is *confidence*—a concept we'll explore later in the chapter) or in another person.

Franklin Delano Roosevelt was speaking of faith when he said, "The only thing we have to fear is fear itself." When you don't know what's going to happen to you and it seems as though you're facing terrible possibilities, your power of belief can give you hope and courage. Strong faith can even help you feel certain that your situation will improve, and this assurance will affect your circumstances.

For many years, I was anxious about money. I was self-employed and a single mom with a child to support. I couldn't prove to myself or anyone else that clients would continue to call me, or that prosperity would flow in and give me enough money to take care of my basic needs, much less provide the lifestyle I wanted to build for myself and my little boy. However, I learned to increase my faith in my ability to make the necessary money to live the life of my dreams, and the result was prosperity and abundance. Today I would say that I have an unwavering *faith* in prosperity and abundance. I don't just *believe* that I am, and will continue to be, prosperous—I *know* that money always flows into my life and that I'm always connected to the abundant supply of the universe.

This belief didn't come easily. I had to practice *feeling* the emotion of faith. I also had to discard any old, negative ideas that made it difficult for me to experience it. I let go of unproductive thoughts about money that would prevent me from achieving my financial goals.

When you have genuine faith, you feel content and at peace and are unwavering in your convictions. You aren't threatened by evidence that you could be wrong, because it truly doesn't rattle you. You feel assured that in the end, what you believe will be proven right.

There are many inspiring stories about people who had faith that they'd prove their doctors wrong and heal from cancer or other potentially fatal diseases. Imagine what faith might bring to *your* life.

Bliss

We all want to be happy and even to feel elated or blissful. When you feel pure joy, you experience a surge of positive energy that makes you want to dance, sing, and laugh.

Bliss is deeply healing . . . not just for you, but for everyone around you. What's more, having a high level of happiness opens you up to ideas about how you can assist others. You can help people raise the lever on their joy in simple ways: with a smile, a touch, or just a few words.

Bliss is also contagious. My Aunt Alice is one of the happiest people I know. She's vivacious and full of humor, and when she walks into a room, she brings life into it, sending out a pure energy of joy that inspires others to increase their own level of joy. We all want to spend time with the Aunt Alices of the world, who exude happiness from their very pores, but you can experience this rich and uplifting feeling whenever you want to—no matter whom you're with or what's happening—just by raising the lever on your bliss switch.

Confidence

Years ago when I was a vice president of corporate development, I created a system of evaluation for our employees that was used to determine everyone's yearly bonus. I told my boss that I found it curious that when the employees were measured against the standards of the system I'd developed, very few had performed at the highest level. While everyone had earned a salary and a bonus, only 10 percent had gotten the full incentive that was available to people who met all their performance goals. I asked the president of the company, "If you look at the people in this top 10 percent who achieved the maximum bonus, what do you think they have in common?" Without hesitation, the president said, "Confidence. They exude confidence, so they get results."

Confidence is a belief in yourself and your abilities that delivers to you the things you want. What you desire may not come exactly when you expect it, or in the form you'd imagined, but make no mistake: Confidence is a tremendously powerful emotion that will change your vibration and bring you what you hope for. Don't talk yourself out of feeling self-assured, and don't let anyone else try to either. Only you know what you're capable of and the passion you have for your goal. Your confidence is like a strong tailwind pushing you along toward your destiny.

Confidence will lift you up no matter what the challenge, helping you access all your personal resources. By feeling faith in yourself, you'll be aware of your many gifts and be able to use them to make your situation better. If you've lost your job, you'll remember all your strengths, talents, and connections with other people who can help you find a new and better one. If you've ended a relationship or friendship, you'll know for certain that you'll attract a loving, wonderful partner or friend, and your confidence will draw them in just as if you were a magnet.

Harmony

Harmony is the feeling that you're spiritually connected not only to the people around you, but to everyone on the planet—and most important, to all that's sacred. You're never alone, even when you're the only person in the room. It's true that feeling the need to make conversation or interact with others can sometimes seem draining, and solitude can be energizing (this is especially true for introverts). However, even when you're by yourself, your energetic connection to the sacred tapestry of life is always there, and if you can make yourself aware of that connection, it will infuse you with positive energy. You'll no longer see the walls and doors that separate you from others. You'll understand that while it appears as if we're all individuals, we're no more separate than the drops of water in the ocean that splash upward on the crest of a wave. Each of us is a part of the ocean even as we're a piece of the divine creation.

A sense of connection and harmony is especially important in business. The strongest companies are ones whose employees feel united as a team and inspired to help each other so that each person does his or her best. I often say to my assistant, Debbie (as well as to my clients, colleagues, and the people I've hired to do work for me): "I'm here to serve. How can I serve?" I truly feel that I want to contribute to the situation and to others so that we can all meet our goals.

It's been said that people don't care how much you know until they know how much you care. We all have a powerful need for harmony and a sense of connection to a creative team, whether we're developing a new product or service or simply a sense of mutual passion and excitement. When a group is working together in harmony, people express respect, admiration, encouragement, and joy whenever they interact with each other. Problems are seen as opportunities to become more creative and brainstorm with colleagues, enthusiastically drawing upon everyone's ideas, knowledge, and skills to face the challenge. Businesses and organizations that encourage people to feel a sense of harmony don't just do well—they thrive.

Calm

When you're calm, it's as if you're immersed in a beautiful, still, warm pool of creativity, love, and joy. If you're feeling tranquil and peaceful, you're relaxed but very focused and aware of your emotions, thoughts, and physical sensations. You can observe them without judgment or worry, easily accepting whatever situation you're in. Put yourself in a calm, almost meditative state, and answers and ideas easily appear in your mind because you're open to possibilities.

I feel most calm and relaxed when I'm driving a long distance. I enjoy the steady movement of my car, the warmth of the sun as it shines through the window, and the sight of miles upon miles of forest on either side of the road. I like to listen to inspiring audio books that further enhance my feeling of peacefulness. In this tranquil state, I'm alert and focused—and remarkably creative: Ideas pour forth, and I keep a handheld audio recorder next to me so that I can capture them quickly.

If you want to achieve your destiny but don't know how to go about it, slow down and switch into the emotion of calm. Soon your next steps will be clear to you. On top of attracting opportunities to you, your peacefulness will draw harmonious situations and people to you, which will enhance your ability to remain calm and in a creative state.

Wonder

Children easily access their sense of wonder because everything is new to them. Recently, I took my six-year-old niece for a walk, and she was fascinated by every puddle and creature, from the squirrels to the robins. The son of a friend of mine came back from the dentist's office excitedly talking about how he got to spit into a special sink that constantly swirls water. . . . It's all amazing when you're six! But as adults, we take so much for granted that we can become jaded and forget our ability to experience the awe and wonder in the simple things as well as the great mysteries of life.

Being able to create a sense of curiosity in an overly familiar situation is very important. It's what keeps us asking new questions and making new discoveries. If Steve Jobs had quit experiencing wonder, awe, and curiosity after inventing the personal computer, we wouldn't have iPods. Great musical artists who've recorded dozens of albums over the years deliberately turn up the volume on their curiosity and wonder, reinventing their careers again and again and making new music that's just as fresh, original, and exciting as what they created years ago. We never grow too old to be curious and filled with awe.

You can use wonder to think of ways to help yourself choose and maintain positive emotions more easily. If I'm feeling a little sad, I'll let myself become curious about what I could do that might make me feel joy more readily. Turning up your level of wonder also increases your happiness. It's exhilarating and energizing to learn something new or to become intrigued by something that you've always taken for granted.

People can be a wonderful mystery, too. Getting to know individuals from all walks of life is an adventure. I love hearing about people's very different lives and opinions. They remind me of how complex and mysterious the human experience is and make me feel not just curious, but joyful.

Inspiration

Inspiration is a breath of fresh air in a stale situation, a drawing in of divine creativity. When you're inspired, your enthusiasm is running high and your determination is endless because you're continually pulling in ideas and energy that fuels you on your mission, whatever it is. No matter what problem you come across, you find ways to solve it or get around it. You feel stimulated by all that surrounds you and find inspiration everywhere: in something that happens in the street; in a sentence you overhear; in an image you see as you're switching channels on the television; or in a thought that simply pops into your mind, seemingly out of nowhere. I love to hear where creative people get their ideas, because it shows just how many possibilities are out there for us to notice when we turn up the volume on our inspiration.

Inspiration also helps you feel determined. Every idea was radical at some point, but an inspired person (or several such people) believed in it and decided to make it happen, no matter what. Inspiration can be so powerful that it increases your feeling of certainty, and you keep on going despite any obstacles.

Kindness

When you turn up the volume on your kindness, you feel good, making it easier for the people around you to choose to feel kind in return. You radiate a joy and compassion that's infectious. You connect to your creativity and find clever ways to express your wonderful feeling of kindness.

Not all people will allow themselves to be lifted up by your consideration, but you can enjoy how delightful it feels to be kind, regardless. Watch how skilled flight attendants will deal with angry passengers who've just been told their plane is late without being given a reason. If they access their feelings of kindness and sympathy, they can say that they're really sorry for the delay and will try to get more information as soon as possible—and then they'll do so, because they genuinely feel kindness toward their passengers.

Many people think that in the corporate world the only way to get ahead is to be a jerk, but that's simply not true. There are many kind people who rise up the corporate ladder, build successful businesses, and make good money. They treat their clients, customers, employees, and colleagues well; and in return, they receive positive feelings and loyalty.

Any form of service or charitable work is an act of kindness that helps you achieve your destiny because you're helping others achieve theirs. Sharing your wealth, whether it's money or time, with someone who's less fortunate connects you to your positive feelings. When you give, let go of expectations. Be fair and generous without calculating what you'll get in return, which creates a feeling of want. There's an old saying: "Cast your bread upon the waters and it will return a thousandfold." Giving from your heart with kindness will always reap a reward for you: joy.

Abundance

Many people are unfamiliar with the emotion of abundance. It's the feeling that you have everything you need—that you're rich and prosperous in all sorts of ways. Abundance makes you feel expansive and generous, since your cup is overflowing. If you have money, you enjoy it and spend it wisely, because in your emotional state of abundance, you're completely comfortable with having it and using it to create more wealth for yourself and the world. You're grateful for all that you have and eager to share it with others.

No matter what you may think you're lacking at this moment, you can create a feeling of abundance and contentment in your life. You can affirm, "I have more than enough and I always have. I am forever connected to the abundance of the universe at all times, in all ways." When you generate a feeling of abundance, you'll attract it, just as I attracted my dream home. The manifestation of your feeling of abundance may be a huge million-dollar home in the woods that allows you to host weekend retreats for your business clients; or it could be a modest but beautiful, well-laid-out apartment in the perfect location in your city. Next year your needs and your monetary situation may be different, but if you continue to keep your abundance switch in a high position, your finances will be exactly what you need them to be.

Worthiness

The Dalai Lama has said that in his homeland of Tibet, people don't understand the Western experience of low self-esteem. Their religion emphasizes a feeling of connection to other people and to the sacred. Not valuing yourself would be akin to not respecting life itself.

In the West, we're more individualistic—that is, we're focused on who we are, separate from those around us. Too often, we start to compare ourselves unfavorably with others instead of recognizing that we're all one. As a result, we struggle to feel comfortable with who we are and have difficulty embracing our worthiness.

When you feel worthiness, you're at ease around other people even when they seem very different from you because you recognize that we're all one, and there's no reason to be threatened by someone who's unlike you in some way. You feel no need to change yourself or others—except to share your own positive feelings with them in the hopes that they, too, can feel as good as you do. If someone reaches a goal that you'd like to achieve, your response is to admire that person and feel happy for him or her. You also feel great about yourself even if you haven't met your own goals yet, because you don't measure yourself by your accomplishments or your possessions. You don't need anyone to tell you that you're a lovable, worthy person. You have no inclination to boast about your wonderful qualities, and you're able to set healthy boundaries to protect yourself from getting hurt.

Feeling worthiness makes it much easier to have confidence as well as kindness, love, faith, and calm. You don't feel that you have to rush around proving your own worth to yourself or anyone else. You're grateful that you are who you are and have the gifts that you do, and you don't envy those of others. You know that love will find you because you recognize that you're lovable and deserving of the rich relationships you desire for yourself.

Courage

Courage is an emotion that often goes hand in hand with faith. The bravest people are not the ones who never experience fear, but those who, as author Susan Jeffers puts it, "Feel the fear and do it anyway." They make an active choice to switch from fear to faith, and this enables them to turn up the volume on their courage. They're not blind to dangers, but they put them in perspective and forge ahead.

Courageous people speak out when they feel that an injustice is being done. They're comfortable sharing their feelings and beliefs, standing up for others and for what they think is right. They know the risks, but they have faith that they can handle any consequences that come along, convinced that in the end, they'll feel the joy of seeing their goal achieved.

Courage, like joy, is infectious. Everyone wants to experience the enormous sense of triumph and love that comes from being brave. When one person switches into a feeling of courage and expresses it, others are inspired to follow suit. Being the first one to speak up takes tremendous courage, but the ripple effect on others will make it easier to continue being brave.

When you're feeling courageous, you also tap into your creativity, because you're no longer blinded by fear or apprehensiveness. You perceive opportunities, as well as your own resources. One of my clients went through a very difficult time financially when he revamped his freelance business. He had the courage and faith to make the changes that he knew would reward him financially down the road, but he still had to pay his bills in the meantime. He explored how he could use his credit wisely and manage his cash flow, and this gave him the ability to remain afloat even as he was investing his time in projects that weren't going to pay off for many months. When you commit to a course of action, courage allows you to find a way to make it happen.

Spotting False Positive Feelings and Learning from Them

When you're genuinely feeling one of the positive emotions, you don't have any niggling doubts, insecurities, or fears. Your instincts are in agreement with your upbeat attitude; and you feel content, energized, and unstoppable.

However, it's possible to fool yourself into a false positive feeling if you're not paying attention to your gut or to the little voice telling you that something isn't quite right. False positive feelings cover up insecurities and fears. When you sense that your bright outlook isn't genuine because a part of you says, *I don't really feel this way*, then stop. Be willing to lower the lever on your positive feeling and explore the negative side of it. If deep down you're frightened, you need to explore that emotion so that you can let go of the fear and create a *genuine* positive feeling to replace the false one.

Let's say that you're feeling false confidence. You talk positively about your plans and your goals but secretly fear any criticism of them. When someone suggests that your plan might need some adjusting, you may get angry or defensive—or even feel a secret sense of relief, because a small voice inside has been telling you that you aren't confident in your ambitions or your ability to carry them off. Something isn't quite right, and instinctively you know it. Pay attention to your gut feeling, explore it, learn from it, and let it go. Then you'll be able to create a genuine positive feeling.

A client of mine knew that she had to move. Because she worked out of her home and was the mother of two small children, she needed more space than she could afford in the city and better access to good schools, nature, and recreation. She talked herself into relocating to a nearby town and began working toward that goal. However, when she called a mortgage broker to see what kind of a loan she could get for a house, he told her that she wouldn't qualify for anywhere near the amount of money she needed to buy even a starter home.

At first she was very upset, but as she explored her emotions of anger and sadness, she realized that they were covering up the feeling that she didn't want to move to the town after all, even if she could come up with the money. The problem was that she'd been afraid to explore her hidden feelings, because she didn't know of any other options for herself and her family. Now that she had gotten beyond artificial confidence, she turned up the volume on her faith and inspiration switches, tapped into her creativity, and the new solution came to her: She realized that she could move to a city several states away that she hadn't considered before. Exploring her false positive emotions—and the negative emotions that they covered up—helped her make a conscious decision to switch into genuine positive emotions, which empowered her to reach her goal.

Creativity, Positive Emotions, and Destiny

Whenever you switch into any positive emotions, you tap into the limitless source of divine creativity that powers your Destiny Switch. You create the energy to keep going regardless of what obstacles you face, and the answers to your problems start coming to you more easily. In addition, you open yourself up to new ideas and possibilities because your heart is wide-open, and this expands your mind, too. Love causes you to learn, grow, and perceive all the opportunities around you that were hidden when you were engaged in negative emotions.

All of us have dreams that we'd like to see come true, whether we're conscious of them or not. Sometimes we bury our desires because we're convinced that we can't have what we want. This is a big mistake. We really *can* attract the life of our dreams by using the power of positive emotions. The problem is that most of us were taught that to get to where we want to go, we have to figure out *how* to get there and work as hard as we can.

I have nothing against researching, planning, musing, or working diligently—I think that they're all important—but too often, people get stuck in their head and start feeling that no matter how hard they try, they can't make their life into what they want it to be. What they don't realize is that they're caught up in negative beliefs and feelings that are attracting destructive situations and people.

I have a friend who, like me, works hard and is talented and skilled at what he does. But he can't figure out why he has to put in so many hours and spend so much time away from his family to earn the kind of money I do. As I've told him, it's not that he has bad luck or that he's chosen the wrong field of work; it's that he believes he can't make good money and have free time—and as a result, he experiences feelings of want and fear.

When you start with a core belief that's based in fear ("If I don't work evenings and weekends, I won't be able to make good money"), lack ("I don't have the ability to bring in money doing what I love"), or unworthiness ("I don't deserve to have an opulent lifestyle"), you manifest circumstances that validate your negative feelings and assumptions. If you let go of any attachment to how and when you'll achieve your goals, you'll open yourself up to other possibilities.

Fortunately, you can choose to feel positive emotions and let your negative ones fall away. However, it's important to realize just how destructive feelings such as lack, discouragement, and anger can be; learn how to recognize when you're slipping into them; understand what they can teach you; and find out how you can let go of them. In the next chapter, we'll explore the most destructive emotions so that you no longer feel tempted to engage in them, no matter what your situation.

CHAPTER FIVE

Avoiding Destructive Emotions

I love tobogganing. I enjoy the feel of the brisk wind tickling my face and the weightless sensation as I'm zooming down a snow-covered hill. Once, though, I had a very unpleasant experience sledding. I'd heard that the hill I was going to try was terrific for tobogganing, so I positioned myself on a new plastic sled, pushed my mittened hands against the snow, and began my descent.

At first the ride was just a little bumpy, and I realized that I was sledding over some thick grasses that were barely covered by the newly fallen snow. Then, as the sled began moving faster down the hill, the bumps got worse: I felt rocks, pits in the ground, and even a painfully hard cluster of slender tree stumps underneath me. My fear was growing, and as quickly as I could, I rolled off the sled and let it sail to the bottom of the hill without me, banging and bumping all the way. I discovered that I'd not only bruised my rear end and my legs, I'd nearly sprained my wrist, which was throbbing and aching. I was much relieved, however, that I hadn't gotten hurt any worse. I decided to pack up and try another hill, one that offered a smooth and safe ride.

Experiencing negative emotions is similar to tobogganing down a hill. Although we consider anger, fear, discouragement, and the like to be unpleasant, there's often a small part of us that foolishly wants to jump on the sled, thinking we'll enjoy it. We believe that we'll feel good about ourselves if we're "smart" enough to greet a new idea with cynicism, or "honest" enough to judge others as wrong and feel angry at them. We mistakenly assume that giving in to distrust or anger will make us feel empowered. We quickly talk ourselves into our right to be envious, discouraged, or unkind and start down a slippery slope toward increasingly negative emotions.

Surrendering to such dark and ugly feelings doesn't make us feel good about ourselves. Almost instantly, we realize that we don't like how we're behaving and we feel guilty, ashamed, and unhappy with ourselves. We know that we've chosen the wrong hill, and it's a bumpy and unpleasant ride.

The Destructiveness of Negative Emotions

The moment you realize that you've chosen a negative, unpleasant emotion, you need to get off that sled—fast. Negative feelings are so powerful that they can be dangerous to your mental and physical health. They may even affect you at the cellular level, causing disease and premature aging.

In fact, the state of anger, hatred, or resentment is a form of death. If you give in to negative emotions consistently, you can actually die of a broken heart or become so enraged or upset that you suffer a fatal heart attack. Evidence shows that optimistic, happy people live longer and have fewer health problems. Positive emotions can be so powerful that they cause sick people to defy the odds and become healthy again or live longer than anyone would predict by looking at their medical chart.

Negative feelings transform the way you see yourself and your life. You might even convince yourself that there's no hope for change. If you don't jump off the sled of such emotions, you'll find the downward momentum building as you slide even deeper into a negative state. Destructive emotions will blind you to your gifts, blessings, and resources, as well as to the possibilities and opportunities that are available to you. To stop yourself from quickly heading down that bumpy hill, you need to recognize the power of negative emotions and the way in which they work together. You also must learn how you can become more aware of when you've accidentally switched into them, identifying the positive emotions you can experience instead.

Recently, I was at a hockey game with my son, who loves to play even when his team isn't doing very well. The mother of one of the other boys on the team came up to me, introduced herself, and immediately began telling me how awful the coach was. She was furious with him for not putting her son in the game the week before, angry that the game had been lost, and certain that the loss was all his fault and that his coaching had ruined the day for everyone.

As I looked at her, I thought of Pigpen, that character in *Peanuts* who has a cloud of dust and dirt swirling around him all the time. Well, this woman seemed to have a cloud of negativity encircling *her.* Rather than getting pulled into the negative story she was spinning and becoming angry, upset, or disappointed about how the team had done the week before, I decided that I'd continue to feel happy that my son was playing his favorite game and help her see the positive side of things. I chose to trust the coach and experience a sense of harmony with the other parents and kids who were enjoying that night's game and feeling positive. At one point, I started chatting with another mom, who was also very happy and enthusiastic, and I ended up sitting next to her.

By the end of the evening, I realized that the angry and unhappy woman was sitting by herself in the stands. She didn't seem to recognize that everyone had gravitated away from her and her poisonous emotions. How much more enjoyable her evening would have been if she'd chosen to feel the love and joy from the others and to be inspired by the positivity all around her!

As I said before, a little bit of poison can kill, and we often underestimate how destructive an emotion such as anger can be. Even the negative feelings that seem quieter and less powerful—for example, worthlessness and hopelessness—can have devastating effects.

You're verbally abusing yourself if you tell yourself, *I'm a loser and a failure. Of course I'm not married—no one would put up with me. I'm a needy, neurotic mess.* Negative thoughts such as this pull down the levers of your worthiness and hopefulness switches. You need to get off the slippery slope of discouragement as quickly as you can and start creating feelings of worthiness and hope.

One way to stop the momentum of negative emotions is to notice when you're validating them by thinking, *I have a right to be angry* [or discouraged, unhappy, lonely, and so forth]. You do have a right to experience your negative emotions, but why would you want to exercise that right? What are such feelings doing for you? You can be justified in your emotion and keep on experiencing it; or you can choose a more positive, productive one. Don't give yourself permission to feel awful and start looking for evidence to validate your choice. If you do, you'll end up making a habit of experiencing negative emotions, and you'll even drive away people who are feeling positive ones—individuals who could help inspire you to raise the levers on your Destiny Switch.

The good news is that as soon as you discover that you've chosen the wrong hill to go sledding on, you can stop yourself from descending into dark emotions and attracting more negativity. You can examine why you've chosen to feel a negative emotion and see what it reveals—maybe a thought is driving it, or perhaps you're trying to cover up an uncomfortable belief or another emotion that needs to be recognized and dealt with. Once you've learned what the negative feeling can teach you, you can choose to switch to one that's positive and creative.

Learning from Negative Emotions

If you're willing to look beneath the surface of destructive emotions, you may discover something about yourself that will help keep you from descending into negativity again. As I've said, if you encounter a false positive emotion, it's good to lower its lever and bring yourself into its opposite, negative feeling just long enough to learn what that emotion has to teach you. Sometimes, too, you'll experience negative emotions that cover up other, even more painful ones. Discovering what these hidden feelings are is important because doing so will allow you to consciously switch out of them.

I've created the following chart to help you become more aware of when you're using one emotion to cover up another. It also shows you which positive emotions to turn up so that the volume of your negative ones is lowered.

IF YOU'RE EXPERIENCING:	IT MAY BE BECAUSE:	YOU MIGHT CHOOSE INSTEAD TO FEEL:
Impatience	You're trying to rush matters because you've lost faith in the creative process of the universe. You're narrowing your focus and limiting your thoughts of possibility.	Patience, faith, confidence, calm
Anger	You're fearful of something. You're afraid to let go of your anger because you think that you'll experience pain.	Love, forgiveness, calm
Sadness, depression	You don't believe that you can attract the life of your dreams. You've closed yourself off from accepting or giving love. You're focusing on the negative only and are repeating old patterns. You're feeling unhappy in a relationship or job because you sense that there's a huge gap between your values and those of the other person or your workplace.	Gratitude, appreciation, happiness, optimism
Dissatisfaction	You're looking at what you don't have instead of what you do have. You've lost sight of the many gifts in your life, and you've forgotten or aren't noticing the enormous and endless opportunities available to you.	Excitement, gratitude
Worry, anxiety	You're fearful of something. You're afraid to let go of your anger. You're no longer enjoying your present situation.	Calm, confidence, faith

IF YOU'RE EXPERIENCING:	IT MAY BE BECAUSE:	YOU MIGHT CHOOSE INSTEAD TO FEEL:
Worry, anxiety	You aren't appreciating what's working in your life. You've lost faith. You've forgotten about your many strengths and gifts. You're holding on to false beliefs. Your anger is out of control.	Calm, confidence, faith
Hostility, hatred, resentment	You have deep-rooted emotions that you haven't dealt with. You feel helpless and frightened that further harm may come to you. Another person is in conflict with your values—for instance, someone isn't being honest with you. You have control issues rooted in fear and become uncomfortable and even threatened when someone does things differently from the way that you'd like to do them.	Kindness, love, calm
Distrust, lack of faith, doubt	Your instincts are trying to tell you that this person or situation isn't worthy of your trust. You're not being honest with yourself. You're not being honest with others. You've created false beliefs and destroyed your faith. Your inner voice is sending you a warning and you need to listen.	Faith, trust, honesty, love, curiosity

IF YOU'RE EXPERIENCING:	IT MAY BE BECAUSE:	YOU MIGHT CHOOSE INSTEAD TO FEEL:
Extreme hurt	You're feeling insecure or inadequate and unworthy. You're interpreting someone's actions in such a way that you're causing your own pain. You're forgetting that you, and only you, control your Destiny Switch; people can't hurt you unless you choose to feel hurt by their actions.	Love, confidence, worthiness
Helplessness, confusion, a sense of being lost	You're forgetting or are unaware of who you are, what you're capable of, and what possibilities are available to you. You're fearful that you're not good enough/ talented enough/skilled enough, etc. Your confusion hides feelings of worthlessness, insecurity, or a lack of faith.	Curiosity, confidence, faith
Discouraged	You're allowing negativity in. You need to review your decisions. You need to remind yourself of your purpose in life.	Inspiration, excitement, faith, wonder
Guilt	You're behaving in a manner that's in direct opposition to your values. You feel that you've done something inappropriate.	Love, kindness
Uninspired, unmotivated	You don't have any goals, or you're doing nothing toward achieving the ones you do have.	Motivation, inspiration, wonder, worthiness, faith

IF YOU'RE EXPERIENCING:	IT MAY BE BECAUSE:	YOU MIGHT CHOOSE INSTEAD TO FEEL:
Uninspired, unmotivated	You're fearing failure and feeling unworthy. You've reached a roadblock or obstacle and don't know how to go around it.	Motivation, inspiration, wonder, worthiness, faith
Jealousy	You have a sense of need, and you fear that you can't possibly have what someone else has. You're forgetting what a wonderful miracle you are. You've lost sight of your unique gifts.	Faith, abundance
Loneliness	You've shut yourself off from receiving love. You fear rejection. You lack faith or feel unworthy of love and friendship.	Faith, love, harmony, worthiness

Remember that when you choose to feel one positive emotion, the others tend to increase as well. Even if you were simply to connect to love, faith, or joy, you'd find it easier to switch out of your negative emotions, whatever they are.

While all negative emotions feed into each other and have similar effects on you, let's look at some specific ones and discover what you can learn from them, why you talk yourself into them, and what positive emotion you could choose to feel instead.

Hatred

Hatred is related to anger and is a strong, active emotion that drives people to very destructive behavior because they mistakenly believe that they'll feel more powerful and less frightened if they give in to it. Meanwhile, the object of their hatred may be completely unaware of it and be unaffected by it. Hating doesn't actually empower people; it simply eats away at them. It doesn't give them comfort either, because they don't experience contentment when they're feeling emptiness, or tranquility when they're in the grips of fear.

Instead of feeling hatred, connect to love and you'll also create feelings of kindness, security, and calm. One day I'd just pulled my car out of a bank parking lot when I saw a friend walking down the street. I slowed down to say hi and ask if he wanted a ride, and within a few seconds, the car that had been a block behind me began blaring its horn. The driver continued to lay on the horn as he slowed slightly and drove past me on my left side. Now, I hadn't done anything wrong or deliberately inconvenienced him, and he'd had plenty of time and room to move around me. Instead of getting rattled and feeling bad about myself, worrying about what he thought of me, or giving in to hatred, I simply finished my short conversation . . . which was a little hard to do because the driver was continuing to honk a block away! He was still holding on to *his* hatred long after he'd solved his problem. I took a moment and directed love and compassion toward the driver, who was making a deliberate choice to feel negative simply because I'd cost him a few seconds out of his day. Choosing to experience love instead of hatred made me feel good.

Hatred is *never* okay, even if its object is a politician whom you disagree with or a criminal you read about in the news. This emotion serves no purpose except to cause destruction. It's far more productive to feel inspired to be part of a positive change—or to feel love for all.

Worry

Worry, anxiety, panic, and fear can be very valuable if they alert you to a true hazard. But even if you're in danger, these emotions are meant to be felt for only a few moments—just long enough to make you aware of the situation so that you can get out of it. If you're in a crisis or are threatened in some way, you need to be positive, creative, and clearheaded, so it's important to switch out of fear and into a positive emotion as soon as you can.

A friend of mine experienced a sudden sense of panic as she realized that her little boy wasn't next to her in a crowd. She allowed herself to feel that momentary fear, but then quickly chose to switch into calm, knowing that this emotion would help her think logically and help her be aware of the possible places where he might have gone. As she took a deep breath and cleared her mind of any anxious thoughts, she remembered that he loved to climb steps and she'd just passed a staircase. She quickly ran back in that direction, and in fact that's where she found him a minute later. Her fear served its purpose for a moment, but quickly switching into the more positive emotion of calm helped her think clearly and find her son.

You might talk yourself into feeling fear, panic, worry, and anxiety because these emotions can prompt you to make changes—for instance, if you're afraid of suffering a heart attack, you might be more likely to stick to a low-fat, low-cholesterol diet. However, fear isn't a very good motivator because it can paralyze you. Use more energizing, positive emotions instead to achieve your goal. Of course you want to avoid a heart attack, eat healthy foods, and exercise, but feeling love for yourself and your family can also encourage you to take care of yourself. Experiencing a sense of worthiness and kindness toward yourself is another great motivator for healthy living.

Depression

Depression may seem like a static emotion—after all, when you feel miserable, you don't even want to get out of bed in the morning —but it has enormously destructive energy. It can cause ill health and poison the way you think, creating a darkness so overwhelming that you can't bring yourself to look for a light switch. This is why it's especially important to take the destructive effects of depression seriously. If you feel that you can't do anything about your despair, seek out treatments to help you adjust your body's chemistry. However, if you catch yourself long before you form a habit of depression, you can make a decision to switch to a more positive emotion.

Usually if you talk yourself into justifying feelings of misery, it's because you think that there's an upside of some sort. Being depressed keeps you from taking risks and trying new things; thus, you can steer clear of situations you don't like and keep yourself from having to confront your fear of failure or of the unknown. However, there's no way to avoid risks, and change is the nature of life. It's much better to accept that fact and access your positive emotions to deal with disappointment and challenges.

When you're miserable or depressed, it's very effective to switch to a feeling of joy, even if you start small. Today I'm joyful that it's sunny and warm. I could feel down about the fact that I'm working inside instead of being outdoors, but I'm happy that I've been able to take a few breaks and walk in the sunshine. I'm also glad that I can look out my window at the trees beginning to bud and the violets peeking up out of the lawn. I'm choosing to see things that make it easy to access my joy, rather than creating thoughts that lead to sadness.

Another reason why you can get stuck in depression is guilt. If you lose someone you love, you might feel ashamed to be going on with your life. You could think that it just doesn't seem right to be happy when your loved one is gone. But if you think about what that individual would want for you, I'm sure you'll see that he or she wouldn't wish you to be steeped in misery. The person knows that you're loyal and care about him or her. You don't have to prove it by getting stuck in sadness. You can honor your loved one by embracing life.

Insecurity

Insecurity is related to feelings of low self-worth. When you don't feel good about yourself, you lose faith in your ability to do what you'd like to do. You can become afraid to make a move for fear that it's the wrong one and even start feeling jealous of others because you mistakenly believe that they possess something you can't have. You don't have to be rich, famous, or glamorous to feel grateful, blessed, and prosperous. You simply need to connect to those positive emotions, and they'll manifest positive results.

When you're feeling insecure and want to switch into confidence, let go of jealousy or unworthiness and discard any negative thoughts about your abilities. Connect with a sense of confidence, and you'll start to become aware of the many opportunities and resources available to you. When I was fearful of not being able to make enough money to support myself as a single mother, I knew that I had to turn up the volume on my confidence. I created that feeling using the tools that I'll show you in the last part of this book, and as I did so, I began to recognize my special talents and skills that would allow me to create the wealth I needed to achieve my goals. The more confidence I had, the more I was able to create for myself.

Loneliness

At the root of loneliness is a feeling that you're disconnected from everyone else. You experience a lack of harmony and have thoughts such as *No one thinks or feels the way I do* and *I'm all alone in the world.* You feel distant from the sacred as well as from other people.

You might not realize just how important a sense of connection is. For one thing, it has a tremendous effect on your physical well-being. Studies have found that senior citizens who have a strong sense of community live longer and enjoy better health than those who don't, regardless of all other circumstances. But even when you're alone, feeling a connection to the divine and to all of life will draw loving people to you and inspire you to interact with others in a compassionate way.

When I was single and unattached, it was often difficult for me to talk myself into going to parties and gatherings where I knew that I might be the only unmarried person. I'd think about how different my life was from that of married people and create a feeling of disconnection. After a while, I came to realize that this negative emotion wasn't serving me in any way. Instead, I chose to feel a sense of connection and harmony with other people no matter what their circumstances were. I'd strike up conversations with other parents of children on my son's hockey team or guests at a party and try to form connections. People always responded positively to my attempts to find common ground with them, and I felt a much stronger sense of community than before.

Anger

Anger is a powerful emotion that can wake you up and make you realize that something has to be changed—now. However, if you stay in it for more than a few minutes (or worse, turn it into a way of life), you won't be anywhere near as effective in making beneficial changes as you'd be if you were to switch into a positive emotional state instead. That's because positive emotions cause you to see opportunities and possibilities that you're blind to when you're angry.

One of my neighbors liked to nap in the late afternoon, but the children on our block, who got out of school each day just as she was settling down to rest, would laugh and shout as they played near her window. Rather than getting angry, she chose to raise the lever on her calmness before confronting the children. The next time they started to play, she came out of her house and asked them if she could talk to them for a few minutes. She explained her problem and told them that she understood why they needed to have fun and make noise when she needed to sleep and have quiet. Because she didn't approach them with anger, they responded with calmness and kindness. She asked them if they had any ideas about how they could solve the problem together. Excitedly, the kids began throwing out ideas, and in the end, they decided that they'd play farther down the block for at least the first hour after school.

Although the children are all fairly young, they've been scrupulous about following the rule they created for themselves. This is the kind of solution that comes about when you quickly switch out of anger into a positive emotion before addressing a problem—you inspire others to be loving and creative.

Emptiness

Emptiness, which is the opposite of wonder and awe, is a very static emotion. When you're bored, you feel as if every day is the same and there's nothing that can surprise or inspire you. It's a very bleak emotion, and it prevents you from attracting the life of your dreams.

If you talk yourself into emptiness, it's probably because you're afraid you might look foolish if you embrace new ideas and different ways of doing things. It's only natural to feel awkward at times, whether it's when you're meeting new people or you're at a party and the conversation turns to a topic you know nothing about. But when you turn up the volume on your emptiness, you can become stagnant and feel that your life is just ticking away.

However, when you raise your levels of awe and wonder, amazing things happen. You let go of your trepidation and fear of what other people might think and start to learn new things and try new activities, and this helps you feel excited and vitalized.

A great way to overcome your feeling of distance and disconnection from others is to use humor. Everyone loves to laugh. Carla, a party planner I know, creates "Hello, my name is" labels that have fun conversation starters on them. One might read "Hello, my name is _____ and I have amazing _____;" while another says "Hello, my name is _____ and I always _____." Guests feel inspired to fill in funny answers, such as "I have amazing dachshunds!" or "I always avoid parallel parking," and it helps people switch out of feeling distant, become curious, and start asking each other questions and getting to know one another.

Discouragement

Often discouragement is a short-lived emotion that we choose when we're experiencing a temporary setback. Its purpose is to remind us of our passion for our goals. After all, if we didn't care, it wouldn't be so challenging to stay positive when events don't go according to plan.

Remember that the universe meets your expectations by mirroring the positive emotions you feel, but *it* will determine just how you'll get what you need. You may think that you belong with a particular romantic partner but not realize that there's someone much better for you just around the corner. Later you might look back and appreciate that the Universal Intelligence made a brilliant call.

A mother I know was deeply upset, sad, and discouraged when she discovered that her son had developmental delays. She chose to switch into positive emotions and enthusiastically began to learn everything she could about her child's challenges. She was inspired to reach out to other parents whose children had delays, offering and receiving support and learning even more about her son's issues. Ultimately, she was inspired to write a book on his condition and speak publicly to parents in order to educate and reassure them. She told me that when she'd first found out about her son's problems, she got angry at God, wondering why her child was chosen to have the challenges he did. Now, she explained to me, the divine plan for her and her son's life was very clear to her, and she felt that her family had been enriched by the experience.

When you're feeling discouraged, listless, and uninspired, remind yourself of your goal, reconnect with your passion—whether it's to create a loving, special family or to develop a fulfilling career—and make a point of raising the volume on inspiration. You'll find ways around any obstacle and continue moving forward toward your destiny.

Unkindness

Kindness is a very underrated positive emotion in our culture. Sometimes feeling and expressing it is portrayed as immature or unsophisticated, but being *un*kind is destructive to ourselves and others.

Since none of us want to think of ourselves as truly unkind, we come up with all sorts of excuses for our behavior. For example:

- "I'm just being funny."
- "He's too sensitive."
- "She'll never hear what I said about her behind her back."
- "He deserves it after how he treated me."

Regardless of the excuse, don't choose this emotion. It may hurt someone else, and it will definitely eat away at your positivity and make you feel disconnected and sad. When people around you are being cruel, switch on your own kindness. Say something loving and positive, and watch how others follow suit.

Impoverishment

You can feel impoverished even if you're blessed with good health, a loving family, and material wealth, but if you continue to engage in this destructive emotion, your gifts will start to slip away. You've heard stories of celebrities who "had it all" but squandered it; or lottery winners who ended up broke, alone, and unhappy despite their winnings. This happens because a sense of lack or impoverishment prevents them from hanging on to any blessings that come their way.

Lack also contributes to feelings of insecurity and discouragement, which keeps you from achieving what you want for yourself. On the other hand, if you feel a sense of abundance and gratitude—even when your bank account is empty and you don't have the family, friends, and good health you desire—you can create all that you need.

You may have hidden fears of experiencing abundance that hold you back from switching into positive and productive emotions. I used to be afraid that if I attracted a lot of money, I'd get used to feeling wealthy, and then my fortunes would wane and I'd suffer. I had to learn to accept that change is a part of life and trust that even if I were to lose all my money for some reason, I'd be able to create it again.

Another fear you might have is that if you have more education, a larger bank account, and greater freedom, people you love will become jealous and demand that they get a share. It's true that some individuals don't handle their loved ones' success well, but you can help inspire them to choose a more positive reaction to your good fortune. What's more, your strong feeling of abundance and joy will attract new people into your life who are very comfortable with who you are and what you have.

Then, too, you may have been raised to think that money is the root of all evil, mistakenly believing, "If I have money, I'm taking it away from someone else." This isn't how money works. Money is like a stream of energy that you can direct—it allows you to help others as well as yourself. I've found that as I've manifested greater abundance for myself, I feel more generous, relaxed, flexible, and creative; and I've been able to help other people create prosperity for themselves because I'm so eager to share what I know with them. I have a feeling of expansiveness, and I love to bring ideas and opportunities to others so that they, too, can fulfill their destiny.

Worthlessness

The feeling of worthlessness is so painful that many people bury it deep within themselves and don't realize that they're holding on to it. If you find yourself having negative, judgmental thoughts about yourself, such as *I'm such an idiot!* or *Who do I think I am?* or *Of course I screwed up—I'm a screwup,* it's a sign that you don't feel worthy. Being harsh toward yourself is very damaging.

You may have been raised to believe that if you felt wonderful about yourself, you'd become conceited, but the very opposite is true. Self-centered people don't experience a sense of worthiness or self-love. They may boast and swagger, but these behaviors don't lift them out of their negative feelings about themselves.

When you raise the volume on your sense of worthiness, you don't feel a constant need to have others validate you. You experience a state of grace and are above any mean-spirited criticism. You don't commit acts of emotional violence against yourself, either by saying cruel things to yourself or letting others do so. You can detach from people who lash out at you and feel compassion for them, but you're careful to protect yourself and your ability to stay positive by avoiding them. When you love yourself, you don't tolerate abuse.

Cowardice

Cowardice is the perception that you can't possibly face what you need to and do the right thing for yourself and others. Feeling cowardly tends to go along with feeling worthless, impoverished, discouraged, and insecure—it's a leaden emotion.

One reason why we allow ourselves to give in to cowardice is that at times in life, we face huge obstacles and experience major trauma. I know a man who was laid off from his job when his company went bankrupt. He'd been there nearly 40 years, starting right out of high school. He'd never gotten a college education or developed new skills on the job, and the pension he'd worked for all those years vanished. He was understandably frightened of what would become of him and how he'd provide for his family. However, he recognized that he'd remain blind to the opportunities available to him if he stayed in a negative state, so he turned up the volume on his bravery and determination.

He began to explore what else he might do for a career; and by connecting to these positive emotions, he also tapped into feelings of self-love and worthiness, inspiration, confidence, and abundance. He's on his way to creating a new path for himself and achieving his destiny. I wouldn't be at all surprised if he later looks back on this challenge as the catalyst for a much more fulfilled life.

⌒∞⌒

By now, I'm sure that you're eager to learn ways to switch out of all of these destructive emotions and into positive, creative feelings that will lead you to your destiny. In the next part of the book, you'll find many practical suggestions for how to deal with your emotions in the moment, over the long term, and during times of great challenge.

⌒∞⌒∞⌒∞

PART III

BALANCING EMOTIONS IN ANY SITUATION

CHAPTER SIX

Switching Your Emotions

Every moment that you're alive is one in which you can make a choice about what you want to feel. You can start creating new habits by mastering the art of switching your emotions, a skill that involves a three-step process. When you're ready to actually make the shift into a better, more positive emotion, there are several strategies you can use—alone or together—that are wonderfully effective at helping you make the switch. First, however, let's look at the three steps in this process.

Step 1: Observe

The first step in making an emotional switch is rejecting a disempowering feeling, and you can't do that unless you observe it. You have to be aware that you're in a negative (or indifferent) state.

Because such emotions make you feel bad, you might have developed the habit of ignoring the signs that you're upset. If you can become consciously aware of your negativity, it will be much easier to switch out of it.

When you're feeling a destructive emotion, even if you're not consciously aware of it, you'll probably experience it physically. Your voice may become higher pitched or shaky. You could feel a churning in your stomach or muscle tension in your body. You might find yourself grinding your teeth or clenching your fists. You may be jumpy and skittish or notice that you're breathing quickly and shallowly. Your hands might even be trembling. These physical symptoms can be the result of the stress hormones adrenaline and cortisol coursing through your body because you've switched into a negative emotion.

If you stay in this state for an extended period of time, you may sleep more poorly than usual, experience a change in appetite, or develop psychosomatic illnesses (that is, your symptoms will be very real but they'll have an emotional cause). Some people have conditions that require them to manage their emotions well because negative ones bring on symptoms such as an asthma attack or a rash, so they've learned how important it is to avoid unhealthy feelings.

Negative emotions will also cause you to behave differently. You'll be overly sensitive and defensive and avoid taking risks or doing unfamiliar things. You'll talk more pessimistically, as well as procrastinate, overplan, and obsess about matters because you don't have faith and confidence. You may stop taking care of your health as well as you should.

If you notice any of these symptoms, it's important to stop and observe your Destiny Switch. Be honest with yourself about how you're feeling, and explore any negative or false positive emotions.

Then, too, people who care about you may point out that you seem angry, defensive, sad, or distrustful. If this happens, do your best not to spiral further into negativity and pull down any other emotional switches. Think about what they're telling you that they've observed, and explore whether there's any truth to what they're saying. Your friends and family are concerned about you and don't want you to feel bad. If they do you the kindness of helping you notice your emotions, accept that gift. Try to switch into love and kindness yourself, and then take the time to explore why you keep entering into a negative emotional state.

Step 2: Decide

In any given moment, you have a choice: Do you want to continue feeling the way you do, or do you want to switch?

Your emotional state at this moment doesn't have to determine what it will be a minute from now. Likewise, how you felt yesterday doesn't have to determine how you feel today. Make the switch that you know you want to make.

Step 3: Switch

You can switch your emotions immediately if you choose to do so. No matter how strong the negative feeling you're experiencing, the more you practice observing, deciding, and switching, the more quickly you'll be able to make the transition to a positive emotion, because you've created this healthy habit.

There are a number of very effective strategies for making an instant switch to a positive emotion. All of them are quite powerful, so if you're only familiar with one or two, I encourage you to try the others as well. You can even use more than one strategy at once. I find that it's especially effective to start with Switching Strategy #1 before using any of the others.

Switching Strategy #1: Slow Your Breathing

Research has shown that when you decrease the rate of your breathing, drawing in oxygen with deep, slow breaths, you counteract the physical symptoms of negative emotions, such as a fast heart rate; the release of stress hormones, including adrenaline and cortisol; and (of course) shallow, rapid breathing. You calm your body, which makes it easier to switch into the positive emotion of tranquility.

One way to slow your breath is to round your mouth to moderate your intake of air, and concentrate on your lungs expanding and your chest pushing outward as you fill it. Another method is to close your mouth, press the top of your tongue to the roof of your mouth, and inhale through your nostrils. It will sound as if you're just about to start snoring, because you've restricted the airflow. Breathe this way for several breaths or several seconds, until you feel that your heart is beating at a regular pace; your muscles are more relaxed; and any tingly, anxious feeling in your body is gone. Choose the emotion of calm, and experience it. Then you can ask yourself what else you'd like to feel and begin creating that emotion as well. Remember, the process becomes easier once you've created one positive emotion. If you relax your body and feel calm, it will be easy to turn up the volume on joy, confidence, love, kindness, and so on.

Switching Strategy #2: Get Away

When I'm feeling a negative emotion, I find that it helps to get away from the situation and even the toxic energy in the surroundings (whether I'm creating it or someone else is) by walking outside or into another room. This isn't the same as avoiding a confrontation or running away from your feelings; rather, it's a healthy strategy for dealing with overpowering negative emotions. A change of locale can remind you that your emotions are in your control. Just as you can choose to walk into another room, you can make the decision to switch your emotions. Any negative thoughts that you're creating about your environment—such as *I can't stand this computer!*—will be easier to discard and replace with love if you're no longer facing the person or object that provoked them. Connecting with an emotion of love overall will make you stop feeling hostile toward whatever it is!

A couple I know say that when they get into their car, it's much easier for them to switch out of the panicky feelings they tend to create when they're in a rush to go someplace. Once they're inside their car, they recognize that they've made it that far (even if they're running late), and this reminds them that they have the choice to make the switch. They'll take a deep breath, turn up the volume on their tranquility lever, and ask themselves if they've forgotten anything in their hurry. They've noticed that this is a very effective way of dealing with time crunches and worry.

At work you can take a walk, go to a bathroom (it's better if you can find an unoccupied one so that you can be alone with your thoughts and emotions), or sneak into any empty room. If you can't physically get away, you can escape in your mind by visualizing a change of scenery. Close your eyes, breathe slowly, and imagine yourself on a quiet, sunny beach or sitting in your favorite chair at home with your loving pet curled up on your lap or at your feet. This will make it much easier to turn up the volume on tranquility and joy.

Switching Strategy #3: Nature Meditation

One of my favorite Switching Strategies was created by a client of mine, Jon Meija, and his partner, R.G. They suggest that you go outside and stare at the leaves of a tree for one minute. Allow yourself to become completely engaged in observing their movements. Try it—you'll be amazed by how calming it is. You can also stare at the waves of a lake or the ocean as you sit on the beach.

Switching Strategy #4: Mini Meditation

Meditation doesn't require a pillow, special clothing, a mantra, or total quiet. You can meditate for a short moment no matter where you are, even in a traffic jam when you're at a standstill with car horns blaring around you. All you need to do is close your eyes, breathe deeply, and detach yourself from your thoughts.

You don't have to try to *stop* your thoughts—I have a feeling that only highly trained gurus can actually do that. You simply have to choose not to follow them wherever they might take you. Pretend that your thoughts are clouds floating before your eyes, just like in those TV commercials where a word such as *innovation* or *inspiration* appears and fades as it moves across the screen. Don't create more thoughts about your thoughts, and of course don't form any emotions about them. Just watch them float by.

In a few moments, you'll feel that your body and mind are much calmer. Then you can ask yourself, *What emotion do I choose to feel right now?* and create it for yourself.

Switching Strategy #5: Use Humor

Just like slow breathing, humor has an actual physical effect on the body. When you laugh, you release hormones known as endorphins into your bloodstream, which lifts your mood. Many studies have shown that laughter actually helps the body heal.

When you're feeling upset, cracking a joke will release endorphins and will usually make others around you laugh as well. This relieves physical tension and makes it easier for everyone to shift into a more positive emotion.

Switching Strategy #6: "Snap" Out of It

This strategy may seem a little strange, but it really does work: Wear a rubber band around your wrist. When you find yourself experiencing a negative emotion or creating thoughts that you know will lead to your switching into anger, frustration, or sadness, snap the rubber band against your skin. The little shock of pain will remind you that you want to make a different decision and choose positive thoughts and emotions. As soon as you snap yourself, say: "Okay, that's enough of that. What emotion do I choose to feel right now?" Doing so will create a negative association with destructive thoughts and feelings. You'll actually avoid them because you've trained your mind to "snap" out of it.

Switching Strategy #7: Create a Verbal Cue

Using a verbal cue to remind yourself that you're able to shift out of a negative emotion—and want to do so—can be very effective, because you'll create an association between that cue and the positive action of raising the levers on your Destiny Switch. You might say, "That's enough of that!" "Time out" "Snap out of it" "Stop—rewind" or any other simple phrase that will have the same effect as a rubber band being snapped against your wrist.

Switching Strategy #8: Get Moving

Exercise can help you let go of negative emotions by reducing your immediate stress and shaking off any worry and nervousness. Some people like to do jumping jacks or stretches to stop their mind from creating negative thoughts and their body from releasing stress hormones. I enjoy shaking like a dog getting out of a pool. A friend of mine envisions the negative emotion and any disempowering thoughts attached to it as a cloud of smoke, and she vigorously waves it away with her hands.

If you can, take a short exercise break when you find yourself feeling a static negative emotion (such as sadness) or an active one (anger, for example). Walk briskly around the block, do some yoga poses, or jump on your rowing machine for a few minutes. When your heart starts pumping, your blood circulates faster and you breathe more deeply, sending increased oxygen to your cells. This makes it much easier to turn off negative thoughts and raise the levers on your Destiny Switch.

Switching Strategy #9: Attend to Your Body

When you're tired or eating poorly and ignoring your body's signals for you to take care of it, it's much harder to switch into a positive emotion. If you're feeling negative, notice whether you're hungry, tired, in pain, or physically uncomfortable. Reject your negative emotion, but don't forget to attend to your body's needs as well. If you're hungry, eat a meal or have a snack (for many people, a protein snack is especially effective at helping them quell their hunger and switch into positive emotions). If you're tired, figure out whether you can take a nap or at least rest, and then make a commitment to yourself to practice better sleep hygiene: Go to bed and rise at the same time each day (even on weekends), engage in relaxing activities before retiring, don't work in your bed or bedroom (because it creates an association between *bed* and *mental activity* instead of *bed* and *sleep*), and avoid caffeine. If you're physically uncomfortable or in pain, by all means, address this with a natural-healing remedy right away, but be sure to observe any *patterns* of discomfort and deal with them.

Sometimes negative feelings such as sadness or listlessness cover up a fear that something is very wrong with you physically. Repressing your insecurity and not dealing with your ailment can be very unhealthy. Be honest with yourself about what you're feeling in both your mind and body, and address your physical needs as well as your emotional state.

Switching Strategy #10: Use Positive Music

A great way to shift your emotions is to listen to music that makes you feel positive. You can choose any type that's especially helpful in getting you to connect with a particular emotion, such as confidence or faith. Nowadays it's easier than ever to create your own mix of music that you can easily carry with you wherever you go and play on your computer, car stereo, or personal music player. You might have one mix that you put on when you need to pump up your confidence while heading off to work and another you play on the way home in order to switch into feelings of joy and love.

Music can also help you connect with another person when you listen to songs that you both enjoy. If you're feeling detached from your romantic partner because you've been preoccupied all day, play some tunes you both love and hum along together. If you like to sing, break into song. If you take pleasure in playing an instrument, pull out your harmonica or guitar, or sit down at your piano for a few minutes. I remember Elton John once saying that as a little boy, whenever he'd get angry, his father would march him over to the piano and tell him to work through his feelings by playing. Once he'd start, of course, the sound of the music lifted him out of his dark mood (and I think it's safe to say that this Switching Strategy led him to his destiny!).

Switching Strategy #11: Connect with Someone Who's Positive

Some positive emotions—inspiration and harmony, for example—are even easier to connect to when you have a little help from your friends. When you're having trouble raising the volume on positivity, you might want to call, e-mail, instant-message, or visit someone you know who will help you switch your emotion. Upbeat people are every-where, especially with the availability of high-tech communication. I know a woman whose toddler went into a prolonged, intense tantrum that shook her up, and she phoned a friend several states away to get support. Her friend offered her gentle words and a reminder that "this too shall pass." Within minutes, she went from completely frazzled and crying to calm, hopeful, and laughing.

Switching Strategy #12: Use Your Imagination

To turn up the volume on an emotion, you must actually experience it. In a way, this is the art of acting. By creating an emotion, you make it real and can intensify it simply by using your imagination. The universe responds to the vibration you send out, so if you're feeling prosperous, it will manifest abundance for you. Just as I entered my dream home and experienced it physically to help create the emotional state that I'd feel once I actually owned it, remember that you, too, can use "props" and "scenes" to assist you:

— If you want to feel abundant and wealthy, go to a car dealership and test-drive a Jaguar, or visit the finest department store in town and try on an extremely expensive designer outfit. Imagine that you own these items. Feel yourself completely comfortable with them. Or visualize yourself setting up the office for your new business. Create a picture in your mind's eye of your business card, with your name and title along with the name of the company. Go to the lobby of a luxury hotel and imagine that you're a guest there.

— If you want to feel confident, visualize yourself on television being interviewed about your amazing success. Stand on an empty stage and picture yourself in front of a roomful of people applauding your speech or performance. Feel the pride at your accomplishment.

— If you want to experience the harmony and love of a romantic partner, imagine yourself with such a person, sharing a special moment. Sit in a candlelit restaurant or another romantic spot, savor the emotion of being deeply connected and intimate, and know that the universe is aligning with your feeling to manifest the partner you desire.

Keep in mind that you don't have to share your dreams and imaginative scenarios with others if you don't want to. Step into the person you know you'll be—and into the life of your dreams—and don't feel that you have to share what's going on inside you emotionally with anyone who won't be supportive of you.

Switching Strategy #13: Use Your Memory

As I said earlier in the book, when we're children, we have an enormous capacity for pretending, and the feelings we create are very real. If you recall that as a child you felt a positive emotion that was particularly strong, re-create it through a memory. Reconnect with the person you were and what you experienced. Ask yourself the following questions:

- What emotion would I like to experience?
- When in my life did I feel that emotion?

Go to a quiet place if you can, and close your eyes. Breathe slowly and deeply as you replay in your mind the scene from your past. Reconnect with that positive feeling and hold on to it. Remember that you're still the same person and can feel that emotion anytime you want to.

One of my clients, who hadn't done public speaking in years and had to give an important presentation, relived his memory of reciting a poem in front of his peers as a child. He reexperienced the tremendous pride, confidence, and joy he'd felt on that occasion. He revisited this memory several times daily for a few days—and then, just before he stepped onto the stage for his big presentation, he closed his eyes and reconnected with it again. The strong positive emotions he created resulted in a wonderfully successful speech.

As you're remembering this scene from your past, if you recall that someone cut you off from feeling good, rewrite the memory in a more positive way. For instance, let's say that you took great pride in a drawing you made and felt very confident about your artistic abilities, but when you showed your work of art to your parent, he or she said something negative. Rewrite this memory as if it were a movie and you were the writer and director. How would you want the scene to play out? Relive it again . . . only this time, imagine the positive outcome of people validating your feelings.

Switching Strategy #14: Reach Out

When you sense that your positive emotions are at a low level or that you're indifferent or negative, a great way to switch is to reach out to help someone else. You'll create feelings of love, joy, and compassion when you choose to engage in an act of kindness, no matter how small.

Good deeds don't have to be grand or well planned. Simply having a cup of coffee with a friend or e-mailing someone an article that you know he or she would enjoy will help a person you care about experience your kindness and connect to his or her own positive feelings. I get a kick out of performing random acts of kindness for strangers, too. From time to time, I'll pay for a drink for the car behind me at a coffee shop's drive-through. Although I never met the person who's getting the free coffee and the clerks are often confused by my request, this action makes me feel great.

Switching Strategy #15:
Replace Negative Thoughts with Positive Ones

Changing your thoughts is another great way to switch your emotions. Although you don't realize it, often your feelings are driven by conscious or even unconscious thoughts. Again, remember the Observe-Decide-Switch approach to shifting your emotions.

Observe whatever negative feelings you're experiencing, but also notice any thoughts that might be driving them. Ask yourself, *Why am I feeling this way? What am I thinking?* so that you can more easily bring to the surface any hidden, destructive thoughts. Once you take a look at them, you can consciously decide to reject them, choose a better emotion to feel, and switch into it.

However, as soon as you get rid of one negative thought, another may appear. Managing your negative thoughts can be like that

Whac-A-Mole arcade game. Your mind thinks, *I'll never get this work done by my deadline,* and just as soon as you whack that thought, the next one pops up: *I'm not good at this type of work anyway.* A great way to whack all those disempowering beliefs so that they stop coming up is to immediately replace them with positive thoughts.

— **Say no to "I can't."** One of the most destructive thoughts you can create is *I can't.* As soon as you think it, you've made it come true . . . but if you get rid of it, you open yourself up to innumerable possibilities. Replace the words *I can't* with *I can.* Turn up the volume on wonder and inspiration, and you'll begin to see how you can accomplish what you'd like to do. Think: *I wonder how I can do this?* and *What might inspire me to figure out a way I can achieve this? Where can I get some fresh insights?* Make sure to turn up the volume on trust and confidence as well. Thinking positive thoughts such as *I can do this. How will I make it happen? Where can I get some good ideas for how to accomplish it?* will help you create the positive emotions of determination, wonder, inspiration, and faith.

— **Get rid of judgments.** It's never helpful to judge yourself or someone else. Critical thoughts create negative emotions and lower the switches on all your positive ones. Instead of passing judgment, give up your beliefs about who's right and who's wrong and what people should and shouldn't do. You can't control anyone else's behavior. Condemning others for acting incorrectly and turning your thoughts to how they ought to fix themselves in order to meet your approval simply creates negative emotions. Practice nonjudgment: Accept people as they are, set your boundaries regarding the behaviors you'll tolerate and the ones you won't, and walk away from situations that you can see will just drain you of energy.

Discarding judgment and connecting with a feeling of love is always a great way of dealing with a challenging situation. We've all seen a mother lash out verbally at her child because she's frustrated and angry, and our instinct is to judge her as a cruel and bad mother. But a far more positive way of handling this scenario is to switch to a feeling of love. As soon as you experience this emotion, express it: Look sympathetic and ask if you can help.

Sending the mother love and showing empathy may very well give her the strength to calm herself down and stop mistreating her child, while judging her and frowning at her will simply keep her in a negative state. Once she sees that you're not going to criticize her or express anger, you can gently tell her what you've done in her situation to help her realize that there's a better way to deal with it. Even if you aren't a parent, you can offer some advice, such as "My niece used to ask for everything in the grocery store, and I know my sister would take a deep breath so that she didn't feel so frazzled. It seemed to get her daughter to stop asking for candy."

Judging yourself by experiencing shame and guilt is also destructive. When you realize that you've missed the mark or made a mistake, turn up the volume on forgiveness, kindness, and love. Forgive yourself and choose to move on. If you see a pattern of behavior that you don't like, commit to a program of fixing it. Getting stuck in a mode of blaming yourself or others will keep you mired in emotions such as sadness and anger and prevent you from switching into positive ones that will actually help you solve problems and feel better.

One of the ways you can tell you've slipped into the behavior of judging yourself or others is that you discover you're using extreme statements with words such as *always, all, impossible, no one,* and *never.* Thoughts such as *I'll never find love, No one will ever cherish me,* and *I'll never find a job I enjoy* are all extreme, negative, distorted perceptions. Whenever you hear yourself saying one of these extreme statements in your head, recognize that it's time to shift into a positive emotion, and find an empowering thought to replace it.

— **Remove the labels.** We all affix labels to ourselves and others because we think that it's helpful to categorize people. We see someone on the street and think, *Young, blonde woman;* or *old, gray-haired man.* Many labels are harmless, but some of the ones we stick on ourselves or others are destructive and inspire negative emotions. Labels such as "foolish," "unreasonable," "stick-in-the-mud," and "busybody" need to be peeled off and thrown away immediately.

When you're confronted with other people's difficult behavior, rather than feeling negatively about them and creating a label for them, use positive emotions and language as you interact with them.

(You'll learn more about confronting challenging people in the next secton.) If you realize that you've just placed a negative label on yourself . . . again, peel it off. Turn up the volume on positive emotions—such as kindness, love, and worthiness—and you'll be able to forgive yourself and move on from any mistakes you've made.

— **Use positive language in every possible situation.** Never underestimate the power of positive language to help you and others shift into positive emotions. When someone asks, "How are you?" respond with "Wonderful! Fantastic!" Say it with enthusiasm and confidence. When I ask people how they are, quite often I hear them answer, "Not that bad," and I'll reply, "You mean it's bad, just not *that* bad?" Then they begin to think about how they really feel, and whether they want to be in that emotional state. Be creative in using positive language, and have fun with it. Not long ago I met up with a fellow golfer at the course clubhouse, just as we were both about to tee off. I inquired, "So how are you feeling today?" He responded, "If I had a tail, I'd wag it." I love it!

Dealing with the Challenge of Negative People

Now that you've learned many strategies for switching your emotions immediately, you're better prepared to create the feelings that you want to experience. You know now that turning up the volume on any positive emotion will empower you and make you feel good.

However, one of the big challenges you'll face again and again is dealing with negative people. When someone confronts you with a strong destructive emotion, it's especially difficult to remember the Observe-Decide-Switch approach, but with practice you'll get better at recalling this very important strategy.

When you're in a confrontation, observe the emotions you've chosen to feel and depersonalize what the other person is saying and doing. Remember that even if people directly accuse you or call you a name, they're responsible for their own feelings, just as you're responsible for yours. They're making the choice to be angry and judgmental. If you unknowingly hurt someone, of course you want to become aware of it so that you can improve the situation, but getting into an altercation won't help anyone feel better, nor will it allow you to solve problems or correct misunderstandings. Then, too, often you'll be on the receiving end of other people's behavior that has absolutely nothing to do with you—you just happen to be where their negative energy falls. When you're blamed or treated with hostility, stay positive. Be calm, loving, and curious. This alone may help the other person switch into a more positive state.

In the martial art of aikido, if you throw a punch at me, I just duck and let it go by. I don't respond to the negativity. This approach is very effective when it comes to other people's challenging behavior. Don't waste your energy engaging in a fight. Let others experience their emotions without letting yourself be drawn into them. If someone attacks you, try to send him or her love. Doing so can break down any negative emotion and open up possibilities and opportunities for you and the other person.

It may be very difficult for you to feel loving around a sibling, in-law, neighbor, co-worker, or person who cuts you off on the freeway. Turn up the volume on love and you'll feel much better than if you indulged in anger or resentment. You'll also find creative solutions to challenging situations and enable yourself and others to heal.

When your sister comes to a family gathering and says that you couldn't possibly understand her problems at work because you're "just" a stay-at-home mom, you can allow yourself to feel angry or hurt or choose to feel love for your sister. You can have curiosity about why she's so angry, frustrated, or jealous, along with what's beneath your own tendency toward defensiveness. You can listen to your sister vent, ask her questions, and help her get in touch with her own more positive feelings while you connect with yours. She might start to think, *If my sister can be so caring toward me when I'm feeling angry, jealous, and unlovable, maybe I'm not such an unlovable person after all.* She may begin to heal her own sense of insecurity.

Love gives you the strength to depersonalize other people's behavior and let go of judgments about them. Filled with caring for yourself and others, you can express your needs in a compassionate way and inspire others to respect your boundaries and sensitivities. Your love will help *them* create love, and this will assist them in treating you considerately, which will make them feel good.

Choosing to feel and express your love toward a difficult person is always a much more productive and positive way to handle the situation than allowing yourself to switch into negativity. Think about how wonderful you feel when you're deeply in love: The whole world seems brighter because you're feeling expansive and caring. If your neighbor blocks your driveway, you're so filled with love and joy that you don't get upset; you simply ring his bell and ask him nicely to move his car.

Sometimes you'll choose to deal with difficult, negative people, perhaps because they're relatives, co-workers, or neighbors and you don't want to (or can't) avoid them completely. When they say something discouraging, you can respond in a way that helps you connect with your own positive feelings, and that might make them more aware of how negative they're being. They may not be able or willing to shift out of their negativity, but you'll feel positive and empowered when you respond in one of the following ways:

— **Sympathize.** One of the most powerful sentences you can say to someone is "I can understand why you might feel that way" or "I'm sorry that's how you feel." In speaking these words, you're expressing compassion and kindness toward someone who could use some positive energy, without having to be drawn into the person's negativity.

— **Suggest a more positive emotion that they could be experiencing instead.** You can do this in a subtle way. If someone asks me, "Doesn't it make you furious when drivers won't move out of the passing lane?" I say, "No, actually, it makes me curious" or "No, it makes me wonder why they're so oblivious to the traffic around them." When a person asked me recently if I was upset that my house hadn't sold yet, I said, "No, I'm not upset. I see it as an opportunity to experience faith. I've priced the house right, houses are selling all over the place, and I know that I only need one buyer and it will be sold."

— **Offer a different, more positive way of describing matters.** If someone complains, "It's so chaotic around here," say "Never a dull moment. I'm glad that we're all able to be flexible and go with the flow!"

— Suggest less extreme ways of looking at the situation. When someone uses extreme words such as *never, always, everyone,* and *no one,* you can gently correct the person's negative distortions, saying, "I can see how you'd feel that way after what happened, but I have faith that not every contractor is a crook."

— Use humor. When someone complains, "I can't believe how impossible the traffic is on this road. I don't know why I even bother getting into my car," you could reply, "I know! Fred Flintstone could pedal faster! Where's our private jet when we need it?" It's hard to stay mad or unhappy when you're giggling!

— Point out the positive aspects of the situation. If someone says, "I can't believe how lousy this hockey coach is," you might comment, "Well, he seems to be able to get the boys to do their best individually and support each other as a team, and I know my son is really having a great time playing with him." If someone else complains about having aches and pains, say, "Well, I'm glad that if you're not feeling well, at least I can be here to cheer you up!" and smile.

— Gently and lovingly point out what others can do to rectify the situation. When people are venting, they usually don't want to hear advice, but after they calm down, often they'll take in and seriously contemplate the words of wisdom they've just been given. When others complain about what's happening politically, say, "I agree that that's a very important issue," and encourage them to write to the newspaper or their local representatives or even run for office. Remind people of their power over their lives. They may not take you up on your advice, but they may start connecting with more positive emotions.

— Emphasize the present moment and the hope for the future. If someone says, "It really stinks that my car had to go to the shop last week," reply, "Isn't it great that it's in the past now?" Then you can switch the subject, saying something along the lines of: "So, what are you going to do now that your car is fixed? Are you going to drive somewhere this weekend just to get away and have some fun?"

— **Remind them of their gifts.** People who see the glass as half-empty can sometimes stop their string of complaints when you remind them of the positive things they have in their life.

Regularly dealing with a difficult person can be very draining because it takes a lot of energy to avoid getting sucked into negativity and keep the switches on your own positive emotions high. If you can, try to delegate the burden once in a while. For example, you can ask a sibling who's less sensitive to your parents' negativity to deal with their needs and give you a break so that you can reconnect with your own positivity.

If the negativity of others becomes so great that you're actually being abused—verbally or physically—and they're unwilling or unable to change their behavior, you must pull away. When you let someone mistreat you, you're being unkind and unloving toward yourself by giving the person permission to abuse you, and that's not okay.

Each time you choose a positive emotion over a negative one, you contribute to a new, healthy habit of being empowered. In the next chapter, you'll learn about tools you can use regularly to keep yourself in a positive emotional state so that when challenges do appear, you can face them with love, curiosity, and confidence.

CHAPTER SEVEN

Creating New Emotional Habits

I hope that you've started to become excited about the possibilities you have available to you and have begun to recognize that you're an incredibly creative and powerful being and can use your emotions to form your destiny. It may sound simple, but it's true . . . and I know it, live it, and witness it every single day.

If you want to create your destiny, you need to form new emotional habits so that positivity is your customary mode of being. You must practice having confidence, inspiration, and faith; and you need to think and act in ways that reflect your positive emotional state. This process is summed up in my favorite quote, from Henry David Thoreau: "If one advances confidently in the direction of his dreams, and endeavors to live the life which he has imagined, he will meet with a success unexpected in common hours." This short quotation is packed full of powerful words, and when followed, it truly is a formula that will help you create and sustain a positive emotional state that will bring about all that you desire. Let's look at the elements involved:

If you *advance,* you're taking action and moving forward. You're actually creating new habits. Every single day you can move toward your goal through action. It doesn't matter whether you're taking small steps or giant leaps forward, as long as you're making progress.

If you advance *confidently,* you're in one of the strongest states of being possible. Confidence is a deeply powerful emotion, and it's within everyone. All you need to do is acknowledge that it's there and begin to experience what it would *feel* like to be confident—and then be it! Confidence is a muscle that becomes strong when exercised. If you have trouble feeling it, use your imagination to practice having this emotion, and it will become easier to keep your confidence switch in a high position.

If you advance confidently *in the direction of your dreams,* you're aware of where you're headed. As I've said before, "If you don't like where you're going, change direction." People have a tendency to go one way and then another, wishing for what they want and then turning their mind in a different direction and thinking about what they *don't* want. As soon as you start thinking about what's undesirable to you, you direct the universe's attention away from your dreams and prevent yourself from moving forward toward your goals. Consider if your actions are taking you in the direction you want to go and whether your thoughts are leading you there as well. Get in the habit of speaking the words and feeling the emotions that will keep you going on the right path.

If you *endeavor to live the life you've imagined,* you actively picture what it will be like when you have what you truly desire. Think about your dream all the time, and feel what it will be like to lead such a life. Visualize yourself already in possession of your goals. Get in touch with the emotions that you'll experience—all of them—and do so often. Endeavoring to live the life you've imagined means acting as if you've already achieved your aims. You can begin this now, no matter how far away your goal may seem.

You'll *meet with a success unexpected in common hours* because you can't know the form or the timing of the success you'll achieve. When you're following the "formula" in Henry David Thoreau's quotation, you absolutely *will* meet with positive results. The universe knows no other way to respond than to provide you with that which you desire. However, the unexpected aspect of success is the "how" and "when." You don't need to know how or when it will materialize—that's up to the universe to decide. Your job is to choose your goal, advance, take action, be confident, and know that the way to your dream will be revealed to you when the timing is right.

In fact, the wisdom contained in Thoreau's quotation is so powerful that I recommend that you copy it and post it in a location where it will be visible to you every day. Read it often, and consider carrying it with you. Remind yourself of the powerful message behind the words. Get into the habit of following Thoreau's formula.

Creating a Habit of Switching to Positivity

When you think of "habits," you might envision the little rituals of your everyday life, such as unloading the dishwasher in the morning or going through your mail as you sit on your front porch waiting for your kids to come home from school. You might not realize just how powerful a habit can be.

Too often people don't pay much attention to their habits, even their negative ones, until someone points them out. You might think that it's no big deal to be in the habit of excessive snacking, but then when you go to the doctor for a checkup, you're reminded of the consequences of overeating, and you realize that every time you reached for cookies and chips without thinking, you were creating a habit. By being aware of this negative pattern of behavior, you can choose to replace it with a positive one. The next time you unconsciously eat a cookie, you can stop yourself and remember that just because you ate one doesn't mean that you now have to resign yourself to being a victim of habit and consume the whole bag. You can put it away and do something healthier than binging on junk food.

Destructive emotional patterns work the same way: You can break the habit of switching into negative emotions or enhancing them by creating disempowering thoughts to validate them. Just stop at the first "cookie"! Then you can create a different habit by consciously making a healthier choice. Soon you'll find that you now have a new, more beneficial habit because you've practiced this so often.

Positive emotional habits are extremely important to develop because they're what will lead you to your destiny. I think the following passage, attributed to Frank Outlaw, sums up the connection between habits and destiny:

Watch your thoughts; they become words.
Watch your words; they become actions.
Watch your actions; they become habits.
Watch your habits; they become character.
Watch your character; it becomes your destiny.

As I've said, I made the mistake of thinking that I ought to be experiencing positive emotions every moment of every day, but I later realized that a better goal is to feel positive as often as possible and develop the habit of switching out of negative emotions quickly when they do arise. The more time I spend in a positive state, the happier and the more successful I am in all of my endeavors. Being enthusiastic, creative, joyful, and loving makes you better at everything—you become a better parent, son or daughter, friend, boss, employee, citizen, and person. You have endless resources available to you because you're tapped into all the wonderful creative emotions inside of you and your hand is on the levers of your Destiny Switch, ready to move any of them up if they slip downward.

You can make the choice every day to put in the effort to create new, positive emotional habits. It's just like exercising: If you start small—even just getting up to stretch a little after sitting at your computer or in front of the television for a while—you'll notice how much better you feel, and you'll be inspired to feel even better. As a writer named Elbert Hubbard once said, "Happiness is a habit—cultivate it."

One of my clients discovered that as soon as she woke up, she'd start to think about all the "problems" she had to solve that day at work and in her personal life. She realized that she'd fallen into a habit of creating negative thoughts and feelings right away every morning. Since she was already accustomed to forming thoughts about her life immediately upon waking, she decided that she could keep this habit but make it a more constructive one. She determined that when she awoke each morning, she'd consciously push aside any negative thoughts or feelings and create positive ones. She'd experience a sense of gratitude as she lay next to her husband and genuinely feel thankful for his presence. Then she'd move on to feel a sense of abundance, picturing all the wonderful things in her life—some of which she'd already made a reality, some of which she knew were on the way to her. Very soon she replaced her old negative habit with a positive one.

Switching Strategies That Keep You Positive

You already learned several strategies for switching your emotions in a matter of seconds. Any one of these can be used not only when you find yourself shifting into a negative emotion—or on the brink of doing so—but also when you're feeling neutral or your positive emotions aren't as strong as you'd like them to be. Whenever you think of it, you can engage in a quick Switching Strategy and raise the volume on one or more positive emotions. When I have a long drive ahead of me, I'll pop in an inspirational-music CD, and almost immediately I'll feel more creative and energetic, so I've made this a habit. I genuinely look forward to long drives, and because I spend so much time listening to uplifting music, books, and lectures, I'm more positive overall than I was years ago. Using quick Switching Strategies regularly will cause you to develop the habit of shifting into positivity.

If you're wondering which strategies you'd like to incorporate into your life, I suggest that you start making a habit of using any of the physical techniques, such as getting up and moving (that is, exercising), practicing deep and slow breathing, and attending to your body's needs. You'll find that not only are you more physically healthy when you habitually exercise, breathe, and take care of yourself, you also feel more positive more often. Many studies have shown that exercise is very effective at preventing depression, and the regular practice of slow, deep breathing makes you less likely to immediately (and without thinking) enter a state of anger and stress.

What we eat and drink and otherwise put into our bodies definitely impacts our emotions. Some people dig their own grave with their mouth, drinking copious amounts of alcohol and sugary sodas; smoking cigarettes; taking powerful medications without questioning whether they're addressing the underlying health issues; and eating harmful, processed foods that strain their body's ability to cope. It's so much more energizing and uplifting to eat a big, nutritious salad with vegetables fresh from the garden than to snack on junk. In addition, drinking fresh water can clear your head, help you focus, and give you a jolt of energy when you need a little perking up. Every little thing you do to improve your physical state will help you stay positive emotionally. If you start with simply meditating for 5 minutes twice a day and going for a 30-minute walk every evening (outside or on a treadmill), you'll see a difference in your ability to keep the levers on your Destiny Switch in a high, positive position.

Serving others is an important habit to develop, because it allows you to make the world a better place even as it raises the level of all your positive emotions. When you take your mind off your own problems and actively get involved in doing something to improve your community (or the global community), you stop sliding down the hill of negative thinking and emotions. Volunteering is one way to help, and nowadays lists of volunteer opportunities are often posted on Websites or in community centers. Many of these activities involve a small amount of time and flexible hours. For example, you might find that a local charity center wants only a four-hour commitment each month to do planting and mulching around their building, or they're looking for people who can devote a few hours a month to serving beverages at a soup kitchen or reading books to the blind.

You don't have to formally volunteer at an agency, either. If you have elderly neighbors, why not clear their walk with your snowblower and check in on them to see if they'd like you to pick up anything from the grocery store? Regularly using the quick Switching Strategy of reaching out—sending articles from the paper to friends, smiling at people on the street, and pitching in to assist someone when an opportunity presents itself—will help you create positive emotions.

You'll probably find that many of the Switching Strategies are ones you've already used, and you know that they make you feel good. But with so many demands on you, you might be telling yourself that it isn't that important to engage in activities that make you feel happy, calm, and inspired. I assure you that it is. Taking a little break to walk outside and look at the leaves or to make a joke and laugh at your situation will make a big difference in your ability to handle life's daily stresses and will boost your positive emotions.

It may have been a while since you spent time doing something joy-inspiring that required planning and effort. If so, recognize that these activities are more than just fun; they're keys to happiness. It's vitally important that you regularly set aside time in your calendar for what you love, whether it's going for a bike ride or reading for pleasure. Upbeat movies that inspire you or make you laugh are terrific for raising the volume on your positive emotions. Books can also help you feel good, whether they're self-help, inspirational, or spiritual nonfiction works or novels that you enjoy.

Don't get into the habit of always pushing aside these pursuits you love in order to attend to obligations. When you sit in the bathtub reading a good novel or pedal along the bike trail for the first time in ages, I bet that you'll think, *I feel so happy doing this! I ought to try it more often!* Well, how *will* you do it more often? What steps can you take to assure that you do what makes you happy? The more joy you experience, the more energy, enthusiasm, and creativity you'll bring to your other activities, from work to doing chores for your aging parents.

Nurturing a Positive State of Emotions

As I've said, to remain in an overall positive state of emotions, you need to create habits that will nurture positivity. Here are some very effective ones that you can create for yourself.

Avoid Speaking Negatively—Embrace Positive Language

Some people are in the habit of using negative language to talk about themselves, their experiences, and their situations. Maybe when you were a teenager you thought it was "cool" to sound flippant or self-effacing and you never changed the way you spoke, or perhaps you got the message from somewhere that if you put yourself down, other people would like you because they wouldn't think that you're stuck-up. Or maybe you were told that you shouldn't "jinx" matters by talking positively and hopefully about what you'll manifest. Whatever the root of this habit, it's important to break it, because what you vibrate, you create.

Let's say that you have a goal, but every time you think about it, negative language pops into your head: You say to yourself, *Yes, that goal sounds wonderful, but what if . . .* or *Yes, I'd like to do that, but I can't make it happen because. . . .* Using words such as *can't, but, hate,* and *never* closes you off from possibilities because they help you pull down the levers on your Destiny Switch and create fear, anxiety, and sadness. Instead of telling yourself, *Yes, I'd like to go back to school, but I don't have the time it would take to do so,* and piling on other worries such as *Besides, it would cost too much money; there wouldn't be anyone to watch my children after school; and I was never a good student, so I'd probably flunk all my classes,* use positive language.

You can open yourself up to your creativity by asserting, *Yes, I'd like to go back to school; and I'd have to find time, money, and child care and learn better study skills.* Have faith that your challenges can be met, and that all your problems have solutions. Don't ask, *Why can't I go back to school?* The universe will send you plenty of reasons if you do! Instead, inquire, *How will I go back to school?* Because your language is in alignment with your intent to reach your goal, the universe will respond to your positivity and optimism by sending you ideas for how to get what you desire.

Do you have a habit of repeating a litany of negative thoughts to yourself, such as *The holidays are depressing because I can't be around my children,* or *Friday nights are lonely, since I never have anyone to go out with*? Remember, situations don't cause feelings. Try to identify these distorted, negative thoughts and replace them with positive ones. This will make it easier for you to let go of your negative emotions, including your powerlessness, and get creative about how to make those times special. You might say, *I'm going to make this holiday joyful by . . .* or *I'll have a great time this Friday night because I'm going to . . .* and see what ideas come to you. As you access your feelings of gratitude and joy, the possibilities will open up. Turn off the negative thoughts, activate the positive ones, and envision yourself having a wonderful holiday and a lively Friday night. Feel love, happiness, and connection.

Avoid Slipping into the Negativity of Others— Uplift Them with Your Own Positivity

As I mentioned in the last chapter, one of the challenges to staying in a positive state is being around negative people. The individual who has the strongest emotional level will tend to pull the other person into his or her own emotional state, unless that other person makes a choice not to be impacted by it and strongly resists.

Not long ago I happened to meet a lovely woman who, like me, was selling her house. We started to have a nice chat, and she told me that she was selling the place because she was getting divorced. It was her second marriage, and naturally she was feeling deeply sad about the breakup. She went on to explain that her second husband and her three sons from her first marriage were having great difficulty getting along, and she'd had to make a choice. She had such sincerity, and I could tell that her heart was aching. Her eyes filled with tears and she started to cry. My eyes welled up, too, and I almost began crying. In that moment, I had to manage my emotions and move to a state of compassion and increase my happiness, knowing that in doing so, I'd help her raise her own level of joy.

She wiped away her tears, and I reminded her of the great things she had in her life, such as her beautiful little boys and her close relationship with them, since they were able to share with her how they truly felt. I told her that after my divorce I'd realized that I was lucky to have had the experience of having my husband in my life, even if it was for a short period, because it gave me the opportunity to cherish and remember the good times. I encouraged her to believe that a new world of possibilities awaits her as she enters this new stage of her life. She started to look up—literally gazing upward as she began to connect with her own faith and optimism—and I could see a smile begin to appear on her face. I was glad that I'd chosen not to be pulled into her sadness. I could still feel a sense of harmony and connection to her and experience sympathy, but rather than commiserate, I'd opted to lift her up . . . and raised myself up in the process.

Sometimes people won't respond to your efforts to help them switch into a more positive emotional state. In such a case, it's okay to simply let them be alone with their feelings until they're ready to make a switch. Several years ago, I was planning on meeting my friend Patricia at a restaurant and going to a concert at the stadium afterward. I was feeling fantastic and on top of the world, and I was very excited about the performance. Patricia showed up at the restaurant and she was in a foul mood. Normally, she's a happy and fun lady, but not this evening—it was probably the worst mood I've ever seen her in.

As soon as we started talking, it was blatantly clear that we weren't vibrating at the same energy level. I knew that I wanted to do whatever I could to help switch Patricia's emotional energy, but no matter what I said or tried to do to uplift her, she was staying firmly grounded in her negativity. I don't think that she was consciously trying to get me to adopt her dark mood, but that's what subconsciously happens when we get into those disempowering states, because we want companionship (remember, "Misery loves company"). However, just as much as Patricia was determined *not* to join me in my positive state, I was equally determined *not* to join her in her negative one. So we had dinner, working our way through conversations that were like a Ping-Pong match: Negative energy would fly across the table, and positive energy would be sent back in the other direction, then the ball would return infused with negative energy, and so on.

When we arrived at the concert, where we had tickets for seats in a box with a dozen other people, Patricia managed to find a chair in a corner and sit down until it began. She now had an "I want to be alone" look about her. I knew that she just needed to be by herself and work through her own emotions, and knowing her well, I had faith that she would do just that. Once the concert began, everyone was on their feet dancing, including Patricia, and it turned out to be a fabulous evening after all.

Of course, sometimes you simply can't avoid dealing with negative people, so later in the book you'll learn more specifics about how you can handle these situations.

Avoid Absorbing Negative Messages— Take In More Positive Information

If you want to hear bad news, it's everywhere—on the TV, on the Internet, on the lips of your neighbor, in supermarket tabloids, and even in the headline crawls on buildings.

Of course it's important to keep informed about what's going on in the world and in your community, but there are ways to get that information without bombarding yourself with negativity.

One of my clients lived in New York City when the 9/11 attacks happened. Afterward, she tried to relieve her anxiety and fear by watching cable-news broadcasts as much as possible. She thought that gathering more information would give her a greater sense of control over her safety and thus help her feel less fearful, even as she woke up each morning to the sound of helicopters buzzing overhead looking for terrorists in the East River and saw constant reminders of the devastation of her city as she walked around town.

One day, however, she realized that watching the news wasn't educating her about the bigger picture of important events as much as it was fanning the flames of her fear about every tragedy and possible tragedy. She realized that by scanning the headlines of the newspaper and reading the in-depth articles that explored problems and their solutions, she felt much better informed and far less frightened. She decided that she'd stop watching TV news and instead read *The New York Times*.

You can pick up a local community paper and find out about all sorts of wonderful people and positive events happening around you. You can talk to neighbors and family members about the people you care about and learn what's going on without getting a dose of negativity along with it.

Even when sad or frightening events occur, we can talk about them in a way that enhances everyone's ability to feel compassion, faith, love, and kindness. After 9/11 and Hurricane Katrina, there were hundreds of heartwarming stories about people who survived, risked their lives to save others, or loaded up trucks full of supplies and took it upon themselves to drive to those in need, offering help. As you discuss the events in your life and in the world, remember to share the positive aspects of every situation with others.

Learn to Be Comfortable with Being Uncomfortable

If you want to nurture a state of genuine positive emotions rather than false ones that cover up your true feelings, you have to accept being uncomfortable at times. Making positive changes can be difficult when you've become accustomed to your old, negative habits. When you start to think, behave, and feel more positively, you may notice that you're uncomfortable, as if you're walking in new shoes. In a way, you are: You're practicing new, positive habits—and you may not be used to that yet, but you will be.

If you're feeling ill at ease, it could simply be because you need to turn up the volume on your faith or confidence. For instance, many people feel awkward at a party where they don't know anyone but the host and hostess. There's no deeper reason for their discomfort than a lack of confidence in their own ability to start up and sustain conversations with strangers. In this case, a little self-assurance and faith will go a long way.

Sometimes, however, your discomfort is a signal that something isn't quite right. If it seems that you should be relaxed and you aren't, take a closer look at your feelings. If you're writing pitch letters to net new clients, you might be nervous because in the back of your mind, you're insecure about your ability to make them effective. Maybe you really do need to hire someone to do the writing for you. If you suspect that your discomfort is telling you that you need to fix something in the situation, listen to its message. Make the changes and do what you need to do to create a positive emotional state once again.

Several years ago I heard the expression "It is better to step forward into growth than to step back into safety." If you're stepping back, it's not into safety—it's actually *unsafe* to retreat from growth. Move forward and embrace change, even if it makes you uncomfortable, remembering that choosing strong, positive emotions will soon become a habit. It will become increasingly easy to switch into a powerful feeling of confidence and faith.

Recast Your "Flaws" as Strengths

If we're to feel love for others, we have to feel it for ourselves, but too often we're very hard on ourselves. Negative self-judgments can be very destructive.

A very common example of such a judgment is looking upon our characteristics as flaws. We may have gotten the message that certain traits are something to be ashamed of, but anything can be a weakness or a strength. To make it into a strength, you need to recognize it, own it, and rethink it.

I'm a person who's very distractible. Rather than judging myself as "bad" for having this characteristic or calling it a "flaw," I've learned to embrace it and be proud of it. The way I see it, I'm distracted by stimulating new ideas that are continually flowing forth from my mind. I've reserved dozens of Internet domain names because I have so many projects that I want to pursue, and these creative ideas are a result of my wonderful gift of distractibility. Now, if this attribute were rooted in a negative emotion such as anxiety, it would be important for me to uncover it and make the deliberate decision to choose a more creative, positive one. Instead, I accept my distractibility, knowing that it's an asset, and I even celebrate it.

Whatever your gifts or talents are, accept and cultivate them. Don't dwell on the characteristics you don't have. This can be hard to do when those around you aren't comfortable with your qualities, but it's very important to stop listening to those negative voices. None of us can be terrifically talented at everything. The greatest partnerships and teams are made up of people with different sets of endowments. In their book *Now, Discover Your Strengths,* authors Marcus Buckingham and Donald O. Clifton list 34 talents that people have—from being a developer, who brings out strengths in others, to being a connector, who puts together people with different talents.

You may not even be aware of all the gifts you have, but if you know what your strengths are, you can foster them. Then if you're missing a particular talent, you can hook up with someone else who has that gift to offer. If you're an idea person, work with someone who has great follow-through. If you're very logical, you can make an excellent partnership with an individual who's more intuitive, because you'll have the best of both worlds. The key is to truly accept yourself—and each other—and make the most of your gifts.

So whenever you start judging yourself for having a "character flaw," turn up the volume on your confidence and worthiness, and recast it as a strength.

- *If you believe yourself to be too emotional,* see yourself as being caring and sensitive.

- *If you're impatient,* think of yourself as a determined go-getter who has a strong desire to get results.

- *If you're a perfectionist,* view yourself as a careful, detail-oriented person with a thirst for excellence.

- *If you're too honest . . .* frankly, you can never be *too* honest. Honesty is an admirable quality, and in this particular case, all you have to do is look upon it as such.

- *If you think that you overanalyze matters,* see yourself as a cautious, reflective, thoughtful person who makes very logical decisions.

- *If you believe that you're too unfocused,* regard yourself as a free spirit who's creative and open to possibilities wherever and whenever they appear.

All of the strategies that you've learned in this chapter will assist you in keeping the volume up on your positive feelings, but I've also discovered several tools that are extremely helpful for developing the habit of being in a positive emotional state. Because they raise the volume on your Destiny Switch, turn up the light in your life, and help you become self-aware, I call them *Illuminators*—and you'll learn about them in the next chapter.

CHAPTER EIGHT

Using the Illuminators

I know that my clients are seeking tools that will help them stay the course as they strive to keep their positivity, create emotions that will aid them in reaching their goals, and get insight into who they are and what passions lie in their heart. That's why over the years I've developed tools that I like to call *Illuminators*. Illuminators are more than just helpful exercises; they're akin to lanterns that will shine brilliantly, allowing you to see the desires that have lain hidden in your heart and lighting the path to your destiny.

If you truly wish to change your life and leave behind the old habits that don't serve you, I hope that you'll do more than just read about these wonderful Illuminators—my desire is that you'll actually use them on a daily basis. Some of them may speak to you more than others, and you might want to begin using those particular ones right away and gradually work in the rest. Make a commitment to yourself to turn on these Illuminators so that you can carry yourself out of the darkness.

Illuminator #1: Your Destiny Switch

You've learned how your Destiny Switch works, but you can benefit greatly from creating a tangible one that you keep in your office or home as a visual reminder of what your emotional state is—and what you'd like it to be.

To create your own physical Destiny Switch, go to any hardware store and purchase a single- or four-switch dimmer panel (or you can photocopy or redraw the one I've provided on page 120, or purchase one at **www.yourdestinyswitch.com**). Start by choosing either a positive emotion that you often have difficulty keeping at a high level or a negative one that you tend to slip into. Let's say that you have trouble staying calm and not getting angry. At the top of the switch, place a label that says "Calm," and at the bottom, affix one that says "Angry."

For 21 days (because that's how long it takes to develop a habit), work with your Destiny Switch, keeping it in sight and moving the lever each evening to mark how angry or calm you were that day. To do so, you must pay close attention to the levels of anger you're experiencing, even if it's painful to be honest about this emotion. If you're feeling a bit irritated, pull the switch just a little toward the anger position. If you find yourself feeling downright furious, pull it much lower.

As you work with this Illuminator, please remember not to judge yourself. The purpose of using it is to shine a light on the levels of your Destiny Switch and on your emotional habits. Each evening, as you record the daily level of emotion you're working with, take a look at how you did in comparison to yesterday. If you did a little better, that's terrific! You probably made a point of being aware of your emotional state and worked hard to keep your switch in a high, positive position. If you didn't do as well, acknowledge that fact, congratulate yourself for observing it, and make a decision to switch into positivity.

It's also good to consider the reasons why you might have slipped a little. Did you forget the Observe-Decide-Switch approach and allow yourself to get pulled into negativity? Looking back, how could you have used one of the Switching Strategies you learned to raise your emotional level? Don't judge or scold yourself. Simply remind yourself of your ability to shift your emotions, and make a commitment to do a little better. The very next time you have the opportunity to make a choice between feeling a negative emotion and a positive one, pick the latter.

Which feeling you work with depends on what you think your biggest emotional challenge is. You might be very aware of a need to develop a particular feeling—such as patience or confidence, for example. Or someone you care about might have told you that you ought to work on a specific emotion. Perhaps you disagree, but consider whether that person might have your best interests at heart and truly want to see you in a more positive emotional state. If others suggest that you seem angry or worried, explore the possibility that you need to focus on creating more calmness or faith. Use your Destiny Switch for just three weeks, noting your levels of these emotions each day, and see what happens.

One of my clients used this Illuminator to discover whether she had a problem with anger, because her partner had pointed out that she was always getting mad. When she heard his observation, she was defensive at first, but then she connected with her feelings of love and trust and recognized that he was truly concerned about her. Although she thought he was wrong, she worked with her Destiny Switch to monitor her levels of anger over the period of a week. To her amazement, her partner was right: She was slipping into anger every day. Working with this Illuminator revealed an emotional habit that she wasn't proud to acknowledge. However, now that she was aware of her anger, she could consciously try to switch it to a feeling of calmness. She also worked on raising the levels of her other positive emotions, particularly love, because as you know by now, all of them work together to lift the levers on your Destiny Switch—and love's power is enormous.

If you like, you can use the following sample Destiny Switch to record what you're feeling. Choose an emotional pair to work with from the Scale of Human Emotions on pages 41 to 42, and write the positive one at the top of the switch and the negative one at the bottom. Each night for three weeks, draw a horizontal lever in the position that reflects your emotional experience for the day, and compare it with what your levels were previously. Notice the movement of the lever over the course of three weeks as you work on using your Switching Strategies to increase the positive emotion.

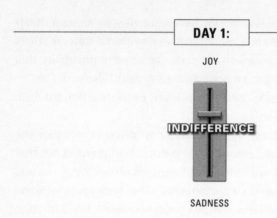

In a notebook, you can draw 21 of these Destiny Switch diagrams so that you can use one daily for three weeks. On each day's switch, be sure to identify the names of the two emotions you're working with, writing in the positive one at the top and the negative one at the bottom.

Illuminator #2: Affirmations

Reciting Affirmations is a powerful way to make your dreams turn into reality. Because you use them to co-create with the universe, it's important that you provide a clear picture of what you intend to draw into your life with its divine help. Remember that you don't want to tell the universe what it is that you feel you lack. If you think that you're in need of something, the universe will respond to your feelings by supporting the fact that you're lacking what you desire. Instead, you want to communicate what belongs to you—love, abundance, joy, and so on.

If you put your Affirmations in the present tense, the universe will recognize what you're experiencing and respond in kind. If your Affirmation is "I will find a romantic partner" or "The right romantic partner will come to me," using the future tense, you're saying that you don't have a romantic partner, and the universe won't bring one to you. To create it, you must vibrate it. You have to feel as if you have a romantic partner already and genuinely experience the emotions of being in love, deeply connected to another person, and engaged in an intimate relationship. Then the universe will respond by bringing you what's in harmony with your vibration. You can create the experience of having a romantic partner by using your imagination and the Affirmation "I am blessed with a wonderful romantic partner"—a statement that's in the present tense.

Many people wonder how specific they should be in affirming what they desire. I believe that it depends on what you want. Maybe you aren't sure exactly what you're looking for. Or it could be that your goal is very definite, and you can firmly say: "I am enjoying my three-bedroom home in my favorite neighborhood, with its big backyard and sunny eat-in kitchen." You can be as specific as you like if it helps you create the powerful emotions associated with what you desire; just remember not to become attached to getting exactly what you want exactly when you want it.

I believe that if your goal is financial, however, it's definitely important to be specific. If you say, "Money is flowing into my life," the universe will bring money to you, but it may not be the amount that you're hoping for. You could get a $3 rebate in the mail, and that would still count. It's better to affirm, "I am making $100,000 this year," or even "I am a millionaire."

If your goal is to create a romantic, committed relationship, I believe that it's critical to open yourself up fully to all of the possible fabulous partners you might meet. You can specify someone who's attractive, has a high-paying office job but rarely has to work evenings or weekends, and loves Cajun music, but maybe you'd be blissful in a relationship with a modestly good-looking person who does meaningful work in the community for little pay and loves jazz. Many people I know have fallen deeply and passionately in love with someone whom they never would have picked out from a personal ad; and they've been in a caring, committed relationship with that person for years.

It's also important that your Affirmations not include any negative language. Don't say, "I am not getting sick this winter" or even "I am not feeling ill," but rather, "I am enjoying excellent health and feel vibrant and energetic." Instead of stating, "I am getting out of debt" and using the negative word *debt,* say, "I am prosperous and have all the wealth I need and more."

Once you've created your Affirmations, commit to reading them with feeling and intensity. Have a full-body experience as you recite them, and truly believe them with your whole heart. It helps if you use emotionally engaging language when you create your Affirmations. I love words such as *opulent, tranquil,* and *vibrant,* because when I say them, I truly feel them. Use a thesaurus to help you find words that not only express what you mean, but which speak to your heart, helping you create their vibration just by speaking them aloud.

Here are some Affirmations that you can use for various occasions:

- *To create prosperity:* I handle and invest my money wisely, and I profit daily. I am a millionaire, and I live a life of opulence.

- *To create enthusiasm and inspiration:* I possess drive, spirit, stamina, and endurance. I have an outstanding winning attitude about myself and everything I do.

- *To create a better body image:* I am in fantastic physical, emotional, and psychological condition. I deeply respect my body and take excellent care of it every day. I experience great pleasure as I enjoy my health and the strength of my physical self.

- *To bring about a job you desire:* My work makes a great contribution to others, and I am richly rewarded for it. I have the ideal career, and I deeply love my job.

- *To create a relationship you want:* I am happy with who I am. People love to be around me because I radiate joy. I am a magnet for all that I desire.

- *To create a feeling of security during a crisis:* My family and I are safe and secure at all times. Many loving people surround me.

Make a point of reading your Affirmations at least twice a day. You can write them on index cards and sticky notes—I have mine on an 8½" x 11" piece of paper, and I keep one copy on my nightstand to read before I go to sleep and another taped next to my bathroom mirror so that I can see it in the morning. As I say my Affirmations, I'm filled with enthusiasm. I smile as I connect to the emotional quality of the words. Remember that how you feel as you speak your Affirmations is the energy that sends your message out into the universe. Make sure it comes through loud and clear! Say the words and believe them with your whole heart and soul.

Illuminator #3: The Power Life Script

The Power Life Script is the blueprint for the life of your dreams, and you're the architect who creates it. It's a description of what you'd be experiencing if you were living your ideal life. I call this Illuminator a "Power" Life Script because it's extremely . . . powerful. I made my first one years ago, and I manifested all that I desired and wrote about. I continue to revise it and work with it every day. I'm creating the life that I've always wanted, and it's thrilling!

To create your own Power Life Script, first write down a list of your intentions. Think of all the areas of your life that you have goals for. What do you want to experience in your relationships? What work do you aspire to do? How do you hope to spend your time? What do you want your health to be like? What financial situation do you desire?

Now, rewrite your goals as an essay, describing what your life is like as you're experiencing it right now. Use emotionally rich language to feed your imagination. You might say, "I feel deeply grateful. My life is flowing harmoniously and magically. I am experiencing great love." Use expressive emotions throughout your script.

Each day you can read it aloud and experience the emotions as you recite it. Better yet, record it and play it back on a portable audio player. I play a recording of my Power Life Script whenever I'm going to be driving (mine is about ten pages long and takes about 18 minutes to read aloud or listen to). It might seem a little strange to drive around listening to your own voice telling you how terrific your life is, but reminding yourself that you have the ability to feel enthusiasm and optimism and can manifest anything you desire is a powerful way to work with the universe to co-create the life of your dreams.

When you first write your Power Life Script, you might not be living it, but listening to it will allow you to act as if you were. You have to step into the script you're creating. You're an actor, inhabiting this role. Soon you'll manifest what you're imagining.

To give you some ideas about how to create your own Power Life Script, here's how mine begins:

I, Peggy McColl, feel the elation and gratitude of easily and smoothly achieving and enjoying all of my goals. All of my success comes easily to me.

I am happy with who I am. I love myself. I appreciate myself, and I treat myself in a loving way. I am love. I express love. I receive love. I am inspired! I am deserving and I am worthy.

I am achieving and have achieved all of my goals and more, and it is all for the greater good. Thank You, God!

I am enjoying being completely healthy in every way: mind, body, and spirit.

I am enjoying a wonderful, beautiful, love-filled, harmonious, peaceful, opulent, joyful, and magical life. For me, every day starts with a warm, happy feeling of gratitude. I wake up knowing that I am very healthy and in outstanding physical condition. I am loved; I am loving; I am surrounded by loving, caring, giving, and wonderful people; and I am thrilled to be so rich in so many ways.

I have an abundance of money in my possession. I have an abundance of money in my bank accounts, and I have an abundance of money available to me at all times.

I am positively serving the world with my gifts and in a way that is beneficial and contributing at a high level.

I walk in the inner silent knowing of the soul because I know that all of my prayers and my desires are already answered, and I feel the reality of this in my heart. I thank You, God.

I attract only peaceful, loving, harmonious people and peaceful, loving, harmonious events into my life.

I am now guided by the wisdom of God in all manners. I ask God for guidance, and He quickly and perfectly responds with the most perfect guidance that provides the most perfect outcome. . . .

I also include Affirmations about my relationships with Michel (my son), Denis (my new husband), my family, and even my dog, as well as about my home and those of my family members, my personal safety, my appearance and health, and any particular goals that I'm focusing on at the moment. I'm often very specific, affirming the wonderful joy I get when I go skiing with Michel and Denis or the delight I take in my landscaped backyard. Throughout my Power Life Script, I continually thank God and express gratitude. Using this Illuminator helps shed light on everything that I'm grateful for and reminds me of all that I have and can create for myself with divine help.

Illuminator #4: The Identity Board

Once you've set your goals, it's important to ask yourself, *Who do I need to become in order to achieve them?* This Illuminator will shed light on what you need to be in order to fulfill your destiny.

I don't believe that people won't or can't change. There are many inspiring stories of individuals who completely altered their lives, going from despair to elation . . . from destructive acts to healing, productive, loving behavior. Don't think for a minute that who you are is set in stone. I always say that if you continue to be who you've always been, you'll keep getting what you've always gotten. To change what you receive, you need to transform your identity. The Identity Board will help you remain aware of the self that you're creating every day as you raise the levers on your positive-emotion switches, make goals and work toward them, and have faith and confidence that the universe is responding to what you're vibrating.

To create an Identity Board for yourself, find a picture frame that has very wide margins or matting. Place a photograph of yourself inside the frame, and using a marker or a label you create, put at the top: "This is who I choose to be" or "Who am I?" Then surround your picture with words that describe what you want to be, writing them on the mat or pasting labels on the frame. Here's a sample:

WHO AM I?

great sense of humor   honest   inspiring

classy   abundantly wealthy   funny

genuine   committed   romantic

courageous   humble   giving   successful

brilliant   radiant   deserving

motivated   spiritual   **(place your photo here)**   vital   worthy

positive   visionary

understanding   friendly   healthy   confident

loving   loyal   dynamic

wonderful   wise   thoughtful   certain   aware

organized   trusting   enthusiastic

knowledgeable   in great shape   peaceful   upbeat

strong

I place my Identity Board directly beside my bed. At night before I go to sleep, I stare at the board and ask myself, *Is this who I was today? Did I demonstrate these states of being?* In the morning when I wake up, I look at my Identity Board again. This time I ask myself, *What am I committed to being today?* and then I say to myself, *This is who I choose to be,* and I read the words I've placed around my photograph. I'm careful to read each one with genuine feeling, connecting to its energy.

Illuminator #5: The Mission Statement

To attract the life of your dreams and achieve your destiny, it's important to be clear about what you intend to create and to regularly remind yourself of this goal. A Mission Statement, which can be long or short, is a declaration of what you believe is your purpose in life. Everything you do and strive for should fit in with this statement. If it doesn't, you know that you're on the wrong track.

My own Mission Statement is this: "To make a positive and beneficial contribution to the lives of millions of others around the world." Every day I look at this statement, which I've printed out and posted next to my bathroom mirror, reading it aloud or silently to myself. It helps me handle challenges more effectively and stay focused, because whatever distractions and problems I've had to deal with, at the end of the day, I know that I've made an effort to live according to my Mission Statement. It puts everything else into perspective.

If you're not sure what your mission or purpose is, ask yourself, *Why was I put on this earth? What am I meant to do?* Think about the types of activities that give you the feeling that you're living the life you were intended to live—allowing you to be true to your values and making the most of your unique gifts. One of my clients decided that her mission was to use her talents and skills to help others express their ideas and beliefs, and to communicate love and compassion whenever she interacted with other people. She fulfills this mission when she teaches creative writing at a community college, as well as in her daily life when she advises others in a loving, nonjudgmental, and compassionate way. For example, when she interacts with friends and acquaintances who are having difficulty expressing themselves at work or in their relationships and are looking for advice, she helps them articulate what their needs and feelings are and encourages them to stand up for and express themselves.

There's no predetermined "mission" or "purpose" for your life. Only you can decide what it is. There is no right or wrong answer.

Use your Mission Statement to help you determine which projects you'll undertake and which ones you'll pass by. When I started receiving requests from other authors and experts to help them get their messages out into the world using my Internet-marketing expertise, I evaluated my decision to offer such a service based on one question: *Was this in alignment with my mission?* Because the answer was yes, I knew that I had to follow through and help them get their voices heard. Supporting them was in alignment with my own mission of making a positive and beneficial contribution to the lives of millions of others. I've been blessed to work with many such experts and authors who have powerful messages that help me deliver on my own purpose. Whether I'm assisting Wayne Dyer in launching his latest book or helping Neale Donald Walsch with the online marketing for one of his titles, I'm living my purpose.

Illuminator #6: The Illumination Journal

Many people keep journals to record their thoughts and feelings of the day so that they can express themselves, as well as look back later and see where they've come from. However, if you write freely in a journal, you may unwittingly start creating negative emotions and thoughts as you jot down what happened to you during the day.

The Illumination Journal works a little differently from a regular journal. Because your entries are succinct and clearly categorized as negative or positive thoughts, beliefs, emotions, or actions, this Illuminator will shed light on any negative emotional habits you've developed. The purpose is not to reveal your destructive thoughts and feelings in order to create guilt, but rather to remind you of your commitment to banish them and replace them with positivity. You need to be aware of your negative emotional habits if you're going to change them.

Find a journal and on the left-hand side of a spread of pages, write a list of all the positive feelings, emotions, and thoughts you experienced each day, as well as the positive actions you engaged in. On the right-hand side, list all your negative feelings, emotions, and thoughts and the negative actions you took. Keep your observations short. The object is to shed light on the number of times you manifest positivity over the course of the day versus the number of times you engage in negativity.

Here's a sample of what a day's entry might look like:

POSITIVES	NEGATIVES
Read my affirmations with conviction.	Got irritable in the grocery checkout line because there was a new clerk at the register who was slow; forgot to Observe-Decide-Switch.
Listened to my Power Life Script.	
Remained calm when I was running late in the morning and even made a joke about it.	
Paid my bills and did so with gratitude for all my prosperity.	Felt guilty for spending so much money on frivolous things.
Remembered to create a feeling of calm and faith when I felt anxious; realized that my daughter would know what to do if I was 15 minutes late picking her up from class; in my calmness, discovered that I could take a shorter route to her dance school and got there only 5 minutes late.	Felt anxious about the thought *What if I'm late to pick up my daughter from her class?* because it took longer to buy groceries than I'd planned.
	Didn't confront my boss about wanting to take a vacation day next week because I was afraid he'd get angry.
Imagined a loving, compassionate way to confront my partner about something that's been bothering me and remained calm, loving, and compassionate while I spoke to him; felt harmony and love when he listened and apologized.	

The more you work with your Illumination Journal, the easier it will be to spot any negative emotional patterns that you need to change. For example, you might notice that you shift into negativity when you're feeling rushed or have to confront someone. Knowing this, you can be more conscious of creating feelings of love, calmness, and faith when you're in these situations.

Illuminator #7: The Daily Challenge

Every morning, read the following questions and answer them aloud. This Illuminator will help you set your course at the beginning of the day, keeping you focused on your goals.

1. What will I do today to give more than I've given before?

2. What will I do today to be more loving?

3. What will I do today to learn and grow?

4. What will I do today to share and create harmony and connection?

5. What will I do today to nurture, love, and express compassion and kindness?

6. What will I do today to bring value to my work, my family, my community, and the world?

7. What will I do today to receive more?

8. What will I do today to believe more?

What I love about the Daily Challenge is that when we make goals, we often set big ones and then forget that every day brings plenty of opportunities—small and large—to carry them out. We all want to be more loving, but in the course of a day you can accomplish this in myriad ways, from smiling at strangers to listening sympathetically to someone who complains to you, offering them love so that they can shift into a positive emotion. You can receive more by choosing to accept a compliment without saying something dismissive or making a joke of it. When you start your day with this challenge to work even harder at being positive, the possibilities of how to do so will be clearly illuminated.

Illuminator #8: The Daily Questions

This Illuminator will remind you why you want to experience certain positive emotions, keeping you motivated to create them whenever possible. At some point during the day, read the following questions and answer them. In your mind, fill in the blanks with whatever feeling you most want to create in your life, or with the positive emotion that you're most likely to overlook. (Remember that all of them are powerful and beneficial, and you may have gotten the message that a particular one isn't useful when in fact it could dramatically change your life if you shift into it.)

1. Why am I now feeling _____ [patience, confidence, inspiration, and so on]?

2. What do I love about my _____?

3. How has my feeling _____ helped me help others and give to the world?

4. What is the greatest benefit of my _____?

5. How will I experience greater _____?

6. What do I need to believe in order to feel _____?

7. What can I do to raise the volume on my _____?

Illuminator #9: The Touchstone Quotation

I've often found that certain quotations perfectly capture ideas that I live by, and each time I read them, I'm reminded of something I know but can lose sight of. One of my favorites is by author Eileen Caddy: "Set your sights high, the higher the better. Expect the most wonderful things to happen—not in the future, but right now. Realize that nothing is too good. Allow absolutely nothing to hamper you or hold you up in any way." In fact, this quote so inspired me the first time I read it that I ran out and bought all of Caddy's books! I've written it on a card that I laminated and carry around with me, and I reread it every day. It's become a touchstone for me.

You, too, may discover that a quotation helps you focus on what you desire and believe, shining a light on your purpose and reminding you of how you want to live. If you find (or already have) a Touchstone Quotation, take it with you wherever you go. When you read it each day, truly connect with what it says. Make it your intention to live by its words.

Illuminator #10: The Goal Card

A Goal Card is a simple reminder of what you most desire for yourself. Each time you read it, you communicate to the universe that there's no separation between you and your aspiration, and the universe will respond by manifesting it for you and illuminating the path to achieving it. You might change your goal when you have a particular concern or challenge, or you might keep it general. I usually work with a Goal Card that says: "I am enjoying being a healthy, happy, wealthy, honest, caring, fun, relaxed, loving, playful, loved, in-love, sweet, and kind millionaire." I keep a laminated copy in my eyeglass case, which is always with me, whether I'm sitting at my computer or going somewhere for the weekend. You might keep a copy posted by your bathroom mirror and dangling from your key chain. The important thing is to have it with you as much as possible so that you can look at it throughout the course of the day.

When you read your Goal Card, make sure that you truly feel the words with all your heart in order to create the feeling of having achieved your objective. Just as with Affirmations or a Power Life Script, be sure that your goal is in the present tense so that in reading it, you don't create a feeling of want or lack.

Illuminator #11: The Life-of-Your-Dreams Experience

You might call this Illuminator a "visualization," but I prefer to refer to it an "experience," because as you visualize, you genuinely experience every emotion described in the exercise along with what it feels like to live the life of your dreams. To work with this Illuminator, set aside at least 15 minutes and make sure that you'll be undisturbed by phones, background noise, or interruptions. Settle into a quiet place and imagine the following. (Note that you can also create a recording of it to play back—if you do, be sure to leave plenty of pauses as you speak so that you'll have time to create powerful images in your mind.)

Close your eyes and relax your body. Breathe in . . . and out . . . in . . . and out. . . .

Continue to relax . . . relax your head and neck . . . feel the tension leave your body . . . you're so relaxed. . . . Your shoulders relax . . . your arms relax . . . your fingertips relax. Breathe . . . in . . . and out. Feel your chest relax . . . your belly . . . your torso. . . . Feel your thighs relax . . . your legs . . . your toes. Breathe . . . slowly . . . slowly.

In your mind, an image is forming . . . the image of your dream life. It plays out with vivid detail, in full color, with sounds and smells and flavors and sensations.

Observe yourself: What do you look like? . . . What are you wearing? . . . Feel yourself inside this healthy, strong, toned, physically fit body. . . . See yourself enjoying the fitness program you're diligently involved in. . . . You love to exercise, you look forward to it, and you do it on a regular basis. If you miss a day, you can't wait to get back to it. . . . Taste the mouthwatering, healthy, nutritious foods that you're blessed to eat each day. . . . You feel the energy of this life-fostering food entering your body as you eat it.

Now, watch yourself as you walk into your new home. Feel the doorknob in your hand as you turn it and open the door. . . . You've now entered your dream home. What do you see? . . . What do you hear? . . . What do you feel? . . . What emotions are you experiencing? . . . Feel the love inside your home . . . the warmth inside your home. . . . Walk through the rooms and observe the splendor that surrounds you. It all belongs to you . . . the beautiful furniture . . . the lovely walls . . . the exquisite architectural features. . . . Feel the support of the strong floor beneath your feet. . . . Drink in the beauty of your furnishings . . . the sunshine streaming in through the window, warm upon your face. . . . Walk over to the window and look out of it. What do you see? . . . It's yours. Savor it. . . . Feel yourself at peace, owning this wonderful home, as you walk through every room. . . . Who is home with you? Who is enjoying this gorgeous environment with you? . . . Who do you love? . . . Who loves you? . . . Connect with the joy you feel, knowing that you're able to spend time with these people. . . . Feel deep affection and security as you imagine these caring individuals in your home. . . . All of you express your love toward each other easily and effortlessly. . . . Feel the unconditional love.

This home is a reflection of your success in your career. What are you doing as a job? . . . See yourself at work, enjoying yourself immensely . . . making the most of your talents and your skills. . . . Success has become a way of life for you. You make it look easy. . . .

Experience how wonderful it feels to be the person you are in your dream life. . . . Your life is complete. . . . Your needs are met even before you ask. You're blessed. . . . You feel blessed, and you offer thanks for all your riches. . . . You give of yourself to others. . . . You feel expansive . . . able and eager to give love . . . compassion . . . kindness . . . money . . . time. . . . You feel grateful for the abundance that you're able to share.

See yourself having a celebratory dinner with your friends. . . . What are you celebrating? . . . Look around the table and see the faces of the many friends who love you . . . the many friends you love. . . . See their smiles. . . . Hear their laughter as you enjoy this magical, joyous evening.

You know that you're living your life on purpose . . . for the greater good of all. . . . You're living your life based on your highest values. . . . You feel tranquil and serene.

People look up to you. . . . You're a leader . . . a true achiever. . . . You know you can do anything you set your mind to. . . . You believe in yourself fully. . . . You're surrounded by family and friends who believe in you. . . . You're a winner. . . . People love to be around you. . . . They experience joy in your presence.

Feel absolute certainty that you've achieved everything you ever dreamed of achieving. . . . Take a deep breath in and feel that sense of absolute certainty. . . . Smile, because you have complete faith. . . . You have an absolute feeling of knowing. . . . You experience the boldness, the genius, the infinite power within you. . . . All the resources you need are inside you, waiting to be tapped into. . . . You have energy and drive. Nothing can stand in your way. . . . You're strong . . . confident . . . more determined than ever. . . . You're creating your extraordinary destiny. . . .

After you've opened your eyes, notice how you feel.

Each time you work with this Illuminator, make the effort to inten-sify the experience. Like an athlete, you can train your body—every cell inside you—to have faith that you can live the life of your dreams. The more often you visualize it, the closer you'll get to achieving it.

Using any of the 11 Illuminators daily will help keep you in a posi-tive state overall, allowing you to concentrate on the emotions that you want to create for yourself. All of the positive emotions are extremely useful, as I've explained, but when you're aiming to achieve a particular goal in life, it's very effective to focus on a few key ones that will help you manifest what you desire. In the next chapter, I'll explain why, and I'll even help you figure out what your goals are if you haven't pinpointed them yet.

CHAPTER NINE

The Four Key Emotions of Your Destiny Switch

As I've mentioned previously, you can be in a positive state overall, but it's highly unlikely that you'll have every one of your positive emotions on full volume at the same time. So, which ones do you concentrate on? I tell my clients that they need to focus on four key emotions to help them achieve the particular goal they're striving to reach.

Four Key Emotions

At all times, we're either growing or dying. Even if you feel happy with where you are in your life right now, you still need to grow. You can aim to be better at maintaining your emotional levels and move forward into an even greater state of joy and positivity by focusing on a particular goal—something that really matters to you—and turning up the volume on the four key emotions that will help you achieve it.

I always suggest concentrating on four key emotions because it takes more than just happiness or confidence, for example, to manifest what you desire. I also believe that no matter what your goal is, you must create high levels of love and faith, in addition to whatever emotions will be especially helpful for your particular aspiration.

Love, as you'll recall, is the most powerful of emotions. It's like a brilliant light that can dissipate darkness and negativity, and it allows people to overcome their grief enough to get out of bed in the morning and dedicate themselves to making the world a better place. My grandmother was practically enslaved as a child, sent by her destitute mother in England to what my great-grandmother had been told would be a better life in Canada. The promise of a warm family and an education was never fulfilled, and my grandmother worked long hours doing manual labor on a farm and was physically abused for years until she finally ran away as a teenager. She made a new life for herself, married a man she dearly loved, and then had to deal with the tragedy of losing newborn twins, as well as her husband a few years later when she was pregnant again.

However, none of these sad events stopped her from pursuing her passion: caring for dogs. She adored them so much that she became the first canine psychologist, traveling the world to help people understand their dogs and have better relationships with them. Her love helped her create a rich and happy life for herself, and it allowed her to give to others so that they, too, could lead a richer life. She certainly had an excuse for feeling depressed and becoming withdrawn, but she chose to experience love instead of sadness. She opted to have faith that no matter what happened, she could create happiness again. What a life she made for herself as a result!

Faith is important, too, because regardless of your goal, you must believe in order to achieve it. You can express your wish to have a particular desire manifest in your life at a particular time, but you must trust that the universe will provide (it always does!), and that it will do so in accordance with its own divine timing.

Let's say you have the goal of going back to finish your college education or to get an advanced degree, but your mind is telling you that you don't have the time or money. The more you try to figure out on your own how you're going to create what you desire, the less faith you feel, since your obstacles seem insurmountable.

But what if instead of attempting to figure it out all by yourself and trying to dictate exactly how and when you get your degree, you simply choose to have faith that it will happen? Using your Illuminators and focusing on faith, love, and any other positive emotions that will help you achieve this goal, you'll open yourself up to all sorts of possibilities you might not have considered. Maintain the belief that the answers will come to you at the right time, and they will. There might be loans or grants that you're unaware of. You could receive money from unexpected sources. Time might open up in your schedule because of events that you couldn't have predicted. This is why it's crucial that you maintain faith that you'll reach your goal even when you have absolutely no clue *how.* You don't have to know the how and when; you simply need to realize that it will happen in the way it's supposed to in due time.

Identifying Your Goals

Of course, to manifest a goal, you need to be aware of just what your aim or priority is. If you're unsure of what you want, ask yourself, *How would I feel if I were living the life of my dreams?* Dream big, and see where your imagination takes you. Pretend that money is no object—that you've won the lottery. Ask yourself, *What would I be doing if I had no obstacles to hold me back?* and *What if I could just wave a magic wand and create the perfect life for myself?* You can explore the question *If I had three magic wishes that I had to use to make my life happier, what would they be?* Close your eyes and visualize where you'd be and what you'd be doing. Most important, experience the emotions that you'd be feeling if you were living the life that your heart desires. What are they?

One of my clients did this exercise and said that he came to the conclusion: "I'd have my own small, cozy cabin in the mountains. I'd be feeling blissful and tranquil, because I'd be out in nature with my family, hiking through the woods and able to stay in my own little place. To me, hiking and being outdoors is deeply healing." My client had rented cabins over the years, so he knew what he wanted for himself, but he'd talked himself out of his dream because he was sure that he couldn't afford it on his salary. Other clients have told me that they can't have what they secretly desire because, as they say, "Who am I to think I could have this? I couldn't possibly create that situation for myself." But you can. My nature-loving client found a cabin priced so low that he couldn't quite believe it at first, but there was no catch—he was able to afford it, and he bought it and has been enjoying it ever since.

Don't be afraid to dream big. The universe doesn't have difficulty manifesting your heart's deepest desire, if that's what it deems best for you. You don't need to do the thinking for it, telling yourself, *Of course it's too much to ask that I have a cabin in the woods, so I'll just ask for enough money to occasionally rent one, because that's a "realistic" dream.* Let the universe decide what's realistic. You may be wonderfully surprised by how it answers the call of your desires!

Opportunities in Alignment with Your Mission

When you have faith that the universe will provide what you desire, it will respond, but you may not recognize its answer at first. If you're not sure about whether to pursue an opportunity that appears to be opening up for you, check to see whether it's in alignment with your mission.

In the 1990s, I was doing some consulting work for an Internet company, and the president loved my ideas and techniques so much that he asked me to become the company's vice president of corporate development. I was taken aback: I hadn't been fishing for a job— I was quite happy with what I was doing. I loved my office, which was located downtown in an old Victorian home and had a working fireplace. I was quite successful running my own consulting business, and I was getting so many referrals that I had no need to advertise. I had to wonder how this opportunity happened to show up in my life. What had I done to attract it?

I considered that maybe the universe was trying to respond to a message that I'd sent out—one related to my purpose and desires. I thought more about the company and my key question was: *Would working for this firm be in alignment with my purpose, which is to make a positive and beneficial contribution to the lives of millions of others around the world?* The company was international, and I realized that its vision *was* in alignment with my mission, so I shut down my business, gave up my beautiful office with the fireplace, and went to work in a cramped office with another person. The job only lasted a couple of years until the high-tech bubble burst, but it was one of the most rewarding careers I've ever had.

What if I'd determined that the job wasn't in alignment with my mission? I would have turned it down, despite the fact that the company offered me a hefty salary and benefits package. The happiest people are those who spend their time in pursuits that match up with their purpose. I've met individuals—and I'm sure that you have, too—who have glamorous, high-paying jobs; beautiful homes; expensive cars; and an exciting social life, yet they're deeply unhappy. That's because they aren't living in alignment with their mission, and no amount of frills and perks makes up for that mismatch between their life and their goals.

Identifying the Four Key Emotions

Here's an exercise that I use with my clients to help them identify the four key emotions they'll need to concentrate on creating if they want to achieve their primary goal.

Name your goal, expressing it in the present tense, as if you've already achieved it. Close your eyes and visualize yourself having accomplished this goal. Stay with this image for several minutes and feel all the emotions that come up. Don't judge them—simply observe them. Now, open your eyes and identify the feelings you experienced. Are they confidence, tranquility, and joy? Are they sadness, worry, fear, and guilt?

If any of the emotions you identified were negative, you need to explore what's underneath them. You may be harboring old, destructive notions in your subconscious that are holding you back from your goal—and if so, you need to consciously discard them.

When you've addressed these negative feelings, name your goal again, expressing it in the present tense, and visualize yourself having achieved it. As positive emotions come up, identify what they are. These are the key emotions that you'll need to create if you want to achieve your goal.

No matter what my goal, the first two emotions that I usually turn up the volume on are love and faith, but you can choose to concentrate on any four key emotions. Your choice will depend on who you are, what your particular challenges are, and what your goal is. I can give you some suggestions, but it's important to look into your heart and discover what it is that you need, because you're the only one who truly knows.

For example, when I decided to start working freelance, I needed a lot of confidence in order to feel that I could make enough money steadily to have the lifestyle I desired. Another freelancer I know, who had a trust fund and plenty of financial security, had great confidence in her ability to make money, but she was very anxious about whether her family and friends would approve of her choice of business. She needed to turn up the volume on worthiness so that she'd make it easier to put any criticism into perspective. Loving herself and feeling faith that the people she cared about would continue to support her emotionally also helped her tremendously—just as valuing myself and trusting that the universe would send me plenty of clients and projects helped me in *my* freelance business. We had the same basic goal, but we chose a different set of key emotions to achieve it.

The following sections describe some typical goals, along with a few suggestions for key emotions you might want to consider focusing on to help you get where you'd like to be. (Remember that if you're trying to figure out which key emotions you personally need to help you with your goal, imagine yourself as having achieved your desire, let yourself experience the feelings that accompany that achievement, and identify them . . . they're the emotions that you want to create *now*.)

Healing from Divorce or Rejection

By now, you know that holding on to anger and resentment because you feel justified in doing so will simply make you unhappy and unhealthy, so no matter how hurt you were by the breakup of a friendship, marriage, or partnership, you recognize that you need to heal and move on. Feeling love for yourself will help you be kinder so that you don't fall into self-judgment and start dwelling on what you might have done differently. Feeling love for the person you parted ways with will allow you to heal your anger and resentment, even if that individual continues to hold on to negative feelings toward you. You'll be very empowered by your ability to send love to your ex-partner or friend.

Having love for your ex doesn't signify that you should rekindle the relationship. Just because you care about someone doesn't mean that you're compatible with him or her. Love your ex enough to genuinely desire happiness and healing for him or her—enough to envision the person feeling genuine joy in achieving what he or she wants in life. The more love you send, the more loving you'll feel, and the easier it will be to heal yourself.

Have faith that you'll create another relationship that's even more fulfilling and rich than the one that just ended. Too often people give in to the fear that they'll never find love again, telling themselves, *I let the right one get away!* Have faith that the ideal person for you is out there. Bear in mind that if you keep your eye on the calendar as you wait for love, you can find yourself slipping into the fear that it will never come. Have faith in the universe, its timing, and its wisdom. Mr. or Ms. Right *will* show up at your door . . . sometimes literally.

Before I met my current husband, Denis, I'd seen him when I was walking around our neighborhood, since he lived near me. Then one day he rang my doorbell and asked me if I could take care of his dog because he was called away suddenly to fly a plane (he's a pilot who's often on call). Our relationship began the day he showed up at my door, and while we were very different from each other—he's quite analytical while I operate from my intuition, and he's very interested in politics while I'm not—I was open to who the universe sent to my doorstep.

My friend Cheryl, who had been unattached for many years, moved to a rural area, which was hardly a hotbed for singles looking for a relationship, but she created love and faith in her life nevertheless. One day the son of the nice older lady next door knocked and asked if he could borrow something, and he and Cheryl have been a couple ever since. Imagine whom you might manifest on your doorstep if you have faith!

A client of mine had ended a business partnership after several years and was fearful of beginning another one. However, by creating faith and love, he was able to forgive his ex-partner and himself for everything that happened and believe that any future partnerships would work out much better—and they did. Faith will also help you remember that you can always rebuild what you've lost, which was my fourth epiphany. If you've formed a loving partnership, you can always create another, and you can choose to have faith that it will be even better than the one you had before.

In addition to faith and love, you might have to create a feeling of worthiness if your self-esteem was affected by the breakup or rejection. You might need to experience a sense of harmony if you tend to create feelings of isolation and disconnection or have trouble reaching out to others and starting and maintaining conversations because you're shy or timid. People who've been fired or laid off often have to make an extra effort to keep their worthiness switch in a high position. If you find yourself falling back into anger again and again, you may also need to focus on tranquility and let calmness reign. Your composure will help you heal, and allow you to attract a new partner who's peaceful and loving.

Starting or Growing a Business

If your biggest goal right now is to start or grow a professional endeavor, love and faith will help you set up a business plan in a way that reflects your integrity and confidence. When I first began freelancing, I wasn't sure what to charge for my services or what types of legal contracts I needed to draw up with my clients. Rather than trying to figure out exactly what I should do to protect myself from every possible disaster and giving in to fear or worry, I accessed my feelings of love and faith, and they guided me. I was able to create agreements and fee structures that I knew honored myself and my customers.

Besides feeling love and faith, you might also want to create determination and confidence to help you. You could even turn the volume up on curiosity and inspiration if you're not sure what kind of business you want to start.

Returning to School

If you hope to resume your formal education, confidence will keep you believing that you'll be able to manage the time demands and financial challenges of going back to school, while faith will point you in the direction of how to do it. Curiosity will help you be open to new ideas and ways of thinking, which will make you a better student. If you allow yourself to experience wonder, you may be inspired to take courses that intrigue you and start creating goals you hadn't considered before. I know a man who took a scuba-diving class in college just because he always wanted to try it. He enjoyed his experience so much that he began doing ocean dives, went on to study marine biology, and now works for an aquarium—all because of one class he took that stimulated his curiosity.

Pursuing a Passion

Your goal may be to rekindle a passion from your past that you want to make an important part of your life again. Love for yourself will help you make the time to pursue the passion that means so much to you. Faith will assist you in finding ways to engage in this pursuit even when your schedule is full. Joy will remind you of just how happy you are when you're crocheting, playing the piano, bird-watching, or engaging in whatever your hobby is, and it will inspire you to devote more time to your passion. Curiosity will help you delve deeper into your chosen activity, learning more and enjoying it more thoroughly.

One of my friends always wanted to play the guitar again, which she hadn't done since college. Creating a sense of curiosity inspired her to check out different types of guitars and guitar music. While she enjoyed playing folk songs on the instrument that she'd owned since college, she realized that she wanted to buy an electric guitar and take some lessons to learn how to play classic rock-and-roll tunes. This new direction in her playing made her feel even more inspired to create time for her hobby.

Healing from an Illness

Choosing four key emotions to focus on can be greatly beneficial when you're trying to recover from an illness. It's very important to have faith that you can heal yourself, because the mind-body connection is extremely powerful. It's also crucial to experience love—for yourself, for the people in your life, and for any medical professionals who may be helping you. Love is energizing, and it will help you when you're having a particularly bad day. Being caring toward those who assist you can keep them feeling appreciated.

You might also choose to focus on gratitude for all your blessings and joy. I knew a man who was diagnosed with (and eventually died of) lung cancer in his mid-50s. I created a Destiny Switch for him, which he ended up carrying around with him wherever he went. I'd labeled little Velcro-backed disks with many different emotions, which he could stick above each of four switches. I learned that the four emotions he chose to concentrate on were faith, love, gratitude, and joy. He trusted that no matter what happened, his family would be okay, and this helped him stop worrying and focus his energy on fighting his disease and enjoying precious time with the people he loved. Whenever he started to feel sad about his condition, he switched into joy, knowing that this emotion would make him feel better and would actually help his body fight his disease.

Because stress can cause and exacerbate many illnesses, you may choose to focus on creating calmness in order to more easily manifest wellness. When you switch into a feeling of peacefulness, you'll put less stress on your body.

Discovering Your Four Key Emotions Exercise

If you're not sure which emotions would be especially helpful to you in achieving your goal, take some time to read the questions below and notice what feelings, images, and thoughts come up.

- How would *love* help me achieve my goal?
- How would *faith* help me achieve my goal?
- How would *bliss* help me achieve my goal?
- How would *confidence* help me achieve my goal?
- How would *harmony* help me achieve my goal?
- How would *calm* help me achieve my goal?
- How would *wonder* help me achieve my goal?
- How would *inspiration* help me achieve my goal?
- How would *kindness* help me achieve my goal?
- How would *abundance* help me achieve my goal?
- How would *worthiness* help me achieve my goal?
- How would *courage* help me achieve my goal?

Allow yourself to sense which emotions you need for your aspiration. Then envision yourself having achieved your goal and notice what you're feeling.

One of my clients performed this exercise, visualizing herself in the perfect house. (She and her family had outgrown the small apartment they occupied; and finding a new, larger living space was her goal.) To her surprise, one of the main emotions she felt as she envisioned her family living in their new home was harmony. She was a person who needed a lot of solitude, and in her current residence—where she had little opportunity to experience privacy—she was creating a feeling of disconnection from her husband and children in order to emotionally create some space for herself.

Rather than waiting until she was able to move into a larger home, she decided to start feeling a sense of harmony right away. By turning up the volume on this emotion, which was one of the four key ones she focused on to get her house (the others were love, faith, and determination), she created joy and inspiration . . . and this influenced her family to feel them, too. With Mom much happier, they all became excited about finding a new home, even though it meant moving away from their neighborhood, and they experienced harmony as they went through the process of relocating.

Your Destiny Switch and the Four Key Emotions Exercise

Once you've identified your four key emotions, start becoming mindful of their levels by working with your Destiny Switch Illuminator, which was discussed in the last chapter. Remember to label each switch and to continue this exercise for at least three weeks in order to instill the habit of consciously maintaining, or even raising, the levels on the positive emotions that you most need in your life at this time. If you like, you can use the following sample as a guide.

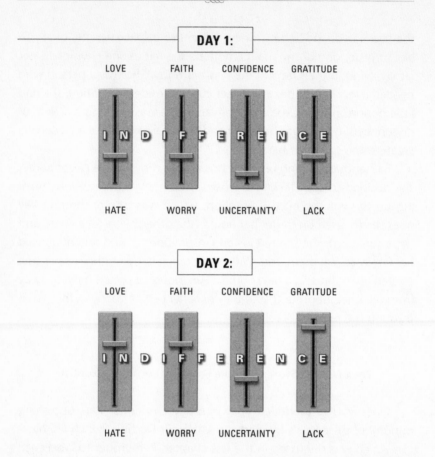

DAY 1:

LOVE   FAITH   CONFIDENCE   GRATITUDE

INDIFFERENCE

HATE   WORRY   UNCERTAINTY   LACK

DAY 2:

LOVE   FAITH   CONFIDENCE   GRATITUDE

INDIFFERENCE

HATE   WORRY   UNCERTAINTY   LACK

Create your own switches in a separate notebook. (Don't forget to label them with your four key emotions and their opposites and to continue using the same ones for at least seven days.)

Now, if your current goal is simply to enhance the life you're living by being more positive overall, you may want to focus on four key emotions that most speak to your heart and will influence all of your goals. There might be particular feelings that you have an especially hard time creating for yourself—feelings that would serve you in many areas of your life. As you choose your four key emotions, listen to your heart . . . you'll know which ones you most need to create.

In the next part of the book, we'll look at especially challenging times, and how you can use your Destiny Switch to manage your emotions in these circumstances so that you can make your dreams come true.

PART IV

GETTING BACK ON TRACK

CHAPTER TEN

Using Your Destiny Switch During Challenging Times

My third epiphany taught me that it's not enough to know what you need to do in order to attract the life of your dreams—you have to actually understand it and apply it. By now, you've learned the Switching Strategies for creating positive emotions, you have Illuminators that can light your way and keep you on track toward your goals, and you've begun developing some positive emotional habits. But what happens when you're faced with especially challenging circumstances?

If you maintain your positive habits, these tough times won't be as difficult, but you'll have to make an even greater effort to keep your emotions in balance than you typically do. Whenever I'm confronted with an unexpected loss or a lot of pressure, I remind myself of how very important it is to use my Illuminators and Switching Strategies. It's easy to let them fall by the wayside when your elderly mother suddenly gets sick and you have to deal with her needs . . . or when there's a crisis at work and you're expected to devote all your evenings and weekends to helping solve it, and tempers are beginning to flare all around you. Yet it's at these times that it's most crucial to use your tools for helping you create positivity and stay focused on your goals.

Let's look at some of these challenging circumstances and see how you can make sure they don't knock you off course.

At Times of Great Loss

The Buddhists say that impermanence is a part of life, and we create suffering when we form attachments. The more we feel that things "have" to go the way we want them to, the more attached we are to how our lives are "supposed" to work out, and the more suffering we create for ourselves. On the other hand, the less attached we are, the less we suffer. When I had my fourth epiphany, I realized that I was creating great anxiety and pain for myself because I was deeply fearful of losing all that I had. I needed to be willing to let go of my attachments if I was going to stop creating negative feelings for myself. When I let go of my need to have lots of money and embraced faith instead, I created the prosperity I wanted and then some.

Occasionally losses are so great that it's hard to imagine how to detach from them. As humans, we can't just decide that despite a great tragedy, we're not going to be sad about it—at all. We have to undergo a process of grief. In doing so, we go back and forth between feeling grief and upliftment, and again and again we're faced with making the deliberate choice to move on. I'm sure that you've had the experience of being depressed or crying and a little thought crept into your mind that said, *I'm ready to stop feeling this sadness now.* In that moment, you made a choice. That doesn't mean that you never felt sad again, but it does mean that you decided to heal.

Each time you make the choice to think, *This isn't working for me right now; I want to experience a positive feeling instead,* you engage in the process of healing. Over time, you'll stop experiencing grief so often; and you'll more quickly switch into comforting, positive emotions.

If you've lost a loved one, I understand that you might feel guilty about moving on and being happy instead of sad. But your loved one would want you to heal from your grief. Make it your intention to work through the process of grieving and healing; and never, ever judge yourself for feeling sorrow . . . *or for feeling happy.* Alternating between the two is part of the process. Each time you notice that you're sad, allow yourself to feel this way; and just as soon as you're ready, push yourself to create a positive emotion through a quick Switching Strategy. As you go through the process, continue to use your Illuminators, and do your best to maintain your positive emotional state.

Remember that negative thoughts create negative emotions. Each time you focus on your grief, you create a sense of loss or lack. However, if you redirect your thoughts to your blessings, you create the feeling of being blessed. If a loved one has passed away and you start to think about the loss, switch into the memory of a wonderful time you spent with him or her. Connect with a feeling of gratitude that you were able to share such an experience with this person and that you had him or her in your life. By creating joy through your memories, you'll draw situations into your life that make it easy to continue feeling this way.

Even if your loss was something smaller—a job, perhaps, or an opportunity for love—don't judge yourself when you find yourself thinking about it and feeling sad or angry. Simply observe, decide, and switch. You've experienced the loss, but when you retell the story of it or replay it in your mind, you relive that feeling. If this emotion isn't making you feel good, then choose another more positive one.

Your instinct may be to talk about your loss in order to keep yourself connected to it. You may want to tell everyone about the horrible experience you had at the job you loved fighting with the new management until you felt that you had to quit. Venting in this way will only make you reexperience the pain and anger. In sympathy, your listener may become angry on your behalf, encouraging you to feel righteous and to keep reliving this story.

But there's another more positive approach to processing your loss. You can describe what happened to you in a more uplifting, happy, and empowering way, either writing it down in a journal or recounting it to others (or both). You can tell people that you had a job you loved in many ways, but one day new managers came in and decided to make many changes. You were challenged to expand your communication skills and develop greater patience, which was a gift because now you'll be able to apply what you've learned in other situations. You used your creativity to find a way to make yourself fit into the new environment but were honest enough with yourself to admit that the wonderful job you had was no longer available to you. You had the grace to accept this reality and the courage to move on.

If you described what happened in this way—using the same facts that were in the negative version of your story but creating positive emotions instead—you'd be well on your way to manifesting a wonderful new job for yourself.

Experiencing Health Challenges

Experiencing a physical challenge is also a form of loss, because you start to think about the level of health you had in the past instead of what you could be creating now. Regardless of whether your condition is treatable, the temptation is to think about it negatively. Your thought may be: *I felt so good last weekend, and this one is shot because I'm sick;* or *I'll never be healthy again if this treatment doesn't work.* The negative thought creates feelings of loss, fear, and hopelessness.

The process of self-healing is similar to that of recovering from grief. If you choose to focus on the disease, you'll continue to manifest and re-create the dis-ease in your body. However, if you focus on health, that's what you'll manifest. In each moment, you can create wholeness within yourself. Remember that your body is making new cells and regenerating constantly, so the new cells that you create can be healthy ones.

The process of visualization—and experiencing the feelings of hope, joy, and contentment that are created when you imagine wellness—is extremely effective for manifesting health. Many, many studies have shown the power of visualizing health, whether it's picturing chemotherapy drugs killing the cancerous cells in the body or envisioning vitality and health returning to injured tissue. By altering your emotions, you change your physical energy vibration, which manifests a healthier body. Dr. David Simon, the author of *Vital Energy,* has said that our bodies are the best pharmacy in the world. We have an extraordinary ability to create health through positive emotions. Holistic healers such as Louise Hay, Deepak Chopra, Bernie Siegel, and Norman Cousins have written wonderful books on this power to regenerate through consistently focusing our thoughts on being healthy.

Handling Criticism

There are people who handle criticism well, taking from it anything constructive that it can teach them, and refusing to judge themselves or feel negatively judged by others. I admire them greatly, since I'm someone who's especially challenged by criticism. Some might say that I'm overly sensitive, but I don't think that it's fair to label anyone in this way. Our level of sensitivity is what it is. And like many sensitive people, I'm a little more attuned to others because of my own vulnerability.

However, I also recognize that it's important to know what my sensitivities are so that I don't immediately pull myself into negative feelings when I'm criticized. Instead, I can stop myself and think, *Oh, that's something I'm sensitive about. Let me be careful to keep a hand on my Destiny Switch here!*

Many times we're exquisitely sensitive because we're still carrying around hurt from our childhood, pain that resurfaces when a similar situation occurs in the present. The way to minimize this sensitivity and make it easier to handle criticism is to be aware of its origins.

I know that for many people, the thought of revisiting painful childhood experiences makes them wince, but we unknowingly relive them anyway whenever someone pulls us back into the recollection of being a child who was criticized, dismissed, ridiculed, or otherwise mistreated. It's far better to bring these memories to the surface and deal with them than to try to stuff them deep down inside ourselves. After all, what we resist persists.

If you're afraid to look at your sensitivities, they'll stay there festering, ready to pop up at any moment. You can't throw your garbage into the trash can, put the lid on it, and not take it out to the curb for pickup. If you ignore that full can of garbage, it becomes very stinky—it doesn't matter that the lid is on tight, because the garbage is still inside. If you aren't willing to look at it, it will stay there and continue to reek until one day the lid comes off and phew! It's not pretty. Either the pain is so great that you completely withdraw, or you "blow a gasket," yelling and screaming and totally overreacting to the current situation. Others will listen to your outburst and think, *Where the heck did that come from?* The answer is that it originated from a stinky garbage can.

Looking at past sensitivities doesn't mean that you have to judge yourself and make yourself feel even worse as a result. The objective is simply to observe and be aware. Once you are, when you feel that garbage coming to the surface, you can recognize that you have the choice to express your negative emotion or release it. You can think, *What I'm hearing sounds like I'm being told that I'm a space cadet, which is what I was called as a child, but I choose not to accept that label. I choose to feel good about myself and curious about what's really happening here.* Wallowing in the garbage isn't going to serve you, but exploring the situation and your sensitivities will. Maybe the other person isn't criticizing you after all, and you'll discover why you tend to negatively judge yourself as a space cadet and how can you recast your "flaw" as a strength.

Again, you can prepare yourself for this challenging situation by being aware, using your Illuminators and Switching Strategies. If you can become conscious of the fact that you get angry whenever anyone gives you advice because being told what to do reminds you of your hypercritical father—or that you feel discouraged whenever you experience a disappointment because you were taught that it's foolish to get your hopes up and have ambition—you can actively choose to discard those thoughts that are driving your feelings. You can say to yourself, *Constructive criticism could really help me here. I'm not going to let myself feel helpless and get upset by this person's opinion.* Making this choice consciously will stop you from sliding down that slippery slope of anger, despair, and discouragement. As Eleanor Roosevelt said, "No one can make you feel inferior without your consent."

In the Midst of a Conflict

Conflicts with other people can cause your body to react instantly with a fight-or-flight response. Without realizing it, you may perceive that you're in grave danger; and your heart will race, your breathing will become shallow, and your glands will manufacture adrenaline and cortisol and release them into your bloodstream to give you quick energy to fight or run. But what your body and subconscious mind is perceiving as the equivalent of a roaring grizzly bear standing over you is rarely a genuine threat of danger. Instead, it may be a misunderstanding or an opportunity for you to learn and grow. In any case, it can't hurt you if you don't let it.

Many books have been written about the challenges of communicating with other people. We have gender, generational, cultural, and personal-style differences—enough of them to keep life very interesting. It's unfortunate that instead of automatically assuming that it's a case of miscommunication when we hear something unpleasant expressed toward us, we usually either feel horrible about ourselves or about the other person. So often what we hear and what was actually said are two very different things!

That's where love comes in. This emotion has the power to pull you back from your primitive response to criticism. It allows you to continue to feel good about yourself and the other person, and to have faith that this conflict will work itself out and the result will be an even better relationship between you.

Take the common example of being criticized by an angry or irritated person. It's very difficult to control your emotions when you're being yelled or sworn at or someone is using heavy sarcasm that's full of rage. Of course, in a circumstance such as this, you're likely to feel attacked and be tempted to fight back.

When I'm feeling attacked, I ask myself one simple question: *What would love do?* I believe that the best thing to do when you're being verbally abused is to send others love or walk away if you have to. I find that it can be helpful to imagine that they are your children and are very frightened, because this makes it easier to create a feeling of caring. If after doing so, they're still abusive toward you, tell them that you choose to feel loving toward them and toward yourself, and that allowing them to abuse you isn't being considerate to either of you (after all, screaming and name-calling simply makes those doing it feel awful as it's happening). Insist that the abuse stop. If you do walk away, keep in mind that you can always continue the conversation later when others are more in control. Let them know that you'll be available to talk when they're able to switch into a more loving state.

If others aren't yelling but you feel hurt as you hear them speak, stop and ask yourself, *Is there a possibility that these words aren't meant to criticize or hurt me?* Genuinely allow yourself to feel curiosity, and open yourself to other possibilities. Ask the person to clarify what was intended.

Remember, too, that people who are under stress and who haven't developed good communication skills will often lash out or be critical or sarcastic, not realizing how destructive these behaviors are. Don't rush to take their words or actions personally! Consider where they're coming from. Are they embarrassed or fearful? Tired or hungry? Not everything is as it seems. Ask yourself, *What else could their behavior or words mean?* You might think of possible causes for their statements or conduct other than an intentional desire to hurt you. Even if you can't imagine what caused others to act in that way, holding on to the thought that the behavior has nothing to do with you makes it easier for you to be loving and compassionate.

Standing Your Ground

When it seems as if you're being accused or attacked unfairly, keep in mind that it's always better to be nice than to be right. When you're nice, you help others create feelings of kindness and trust, and this will allow them to come around to see the situation from your point of view. A friend of mine recently got a message from an angry client who accused him of not doing work that she insisted he'd promised to do. My friend knew that he'd never agreed to any such thing, and that the client—in her panic to meet a self-imposed deadline—had worked herself into a frenzy, which distorted her memory of their conversation. (Of course, this is an example of why it's important to have written agreements!)

My friend could have gotten defensive and angry and lashed out in response. However, my advice to him was to create a feeling of caring and imagine his client being filled with love and gratitude. I explained that when people are in a distrustful state, they may not be able to see the truth, or they make up situations that don't exist, creating their own distorted "truth." I suggested that once my friend had created a feeling of love and visualized sending it to his client, he should call her back, listen with love as she presented her side of the story, and reassert what they'd agreed to.

"But what if she's unreasonable and refuses to pay her bill?" my friend asked. I advised him to be firm, reiterate the reasons why he was owed the money, and insist that she pay the invoice. Being loving but firm can be extremely effective in helping people switch out of their negativity and create positive emotions and a clearer state of mind. If you've been wronged, lovingly and firmly assert yourself!

Accepting and Moving On

Sometimes, however, it's best to just accept a loss and move on rather than engage in a fruitless discussion with people who don't want to switch out of negativity. Wish them well, give them love, and remember that anything you created—whether it was money or an opportunity—you can manifest again through your positivity.

Recently someone I know was sued by his ex-wife for back child support (their kids were grown and had already graduated from college). Now, it isn't as if he didn't support his children—he and his ex-wife had shared custody, and he'd spent money on the kids when they were with him just as she did when they were with her. However, she'd kept meticulous notes throughout the years and presented him with a bill, insisting that he prove he'd spent just as much as she had. Having supported his children lovingly and without any sense of resentment, he'd never thought to tally up what he paid for, and he couldn't prove that he'd matched the amount she'd spent. Since my friend couldn't afford a top-notch lawyer, he lost his case, and the court awarded his ex-wife a hefty judgment.

My friend was beside himself with anger at having to pay his former wife. He had to sell a truck that was extremely helpful to him in his work, empty his meager savings account, and cash in his retirement fund. I told him that while he was justified in feeling anger, the question was: *Did feeling angry serve him in any way?* He admitted that it didn't. It was making him feel miserable and was affecting his new marriage, and he wanted to rid himself of his rage. I reminded him that he'd made the money once and could do so again.

In a case such as this, it can be very helpful to remember that every change and challenge provides us with an opportunity to learn and grow. My friend came to have faith in his ability to re-create anything that he'd already made for himself once before. He learned to let go of his rage and create positive emotions. Realizing that he could accomplish this made him feel very empowered and energized. In time, he was able to take my advice to send his ex-wife love.

Perhaps one day she'll take a look at how she behaved and decide that it wasn't right and make up for it somehow. Or maybe she won't and will spend the rest of her life feeling a sense of lack no matter how much money she has. Nobody can know. But one thing I'm certain of is that by choosing love and its tremendous power, my friend was able to get back on track to his destiny.

Busy Times

We can't always predict when our plates will be overflowing with responsibilities, but sometimes we can. If you know that your schedule is going to become very crowded, decide to keep your commitment to using your Illuminators, even if they might seem time-consuming. Creating positive emotions is always an excellent investment because these feelings will energize you. Plan to take time to focus on positive emotions in any way you can think of.

Holidays are an especially challenging time. In trying to create the mood of the season, too often people overextend themselves. A joyous holiday gathering to bring together family and friends becomes a humongous chore, and the focus on love and harmony gets lost in the search for just the right centerpiece and appetizers. You can decide well before the event how much time you want to devote to taking on more responsibilities and projects, and you can create an oasis for yourself.

I know a couple who would sit down before Thanksgiving each year to discuss how to adjust their home life to accommodate the demands of the next six weeks. The husband worked in retail, and the Christmas season kept him at his store for long hours. Their children were out of school for good chunks of that six-week period, which placed more demands on their mother, who worked part-time. Therefore, they knew that this discussion could help prevent them from going into overload. They planned what they'd do to make up for the extra chores and obligations and the limited time they'd have. Then they deliberately chose ways to celebrate the holiday that would allow them to enjoy it without creating more demands on their time.

One of their holiday rituals was to arrange to have their children stay with their neighbors while the two of them went to a Sunday-morning performance of music from the Middle Ages, a concert series that ran every Christmastime. Sitting in a beautiful, high-ceilinged cathedral, listening to the music resonate around them, helped them create feelings of tranquility, bliss, and harmony. It was a small commitment of time, but each year they looked forward to that little oasis of peace and loveliness in the midst of their busy holiday season.

It's also important to observe the way you talk about hectic times, because you can unknowingly create negative emotions when you say, "Things are crazy around here" or "It's a madhouse at work." It's far more positive to comment, "Things are wonderfully active around here" or "We're superbusy at work! It's a very productive and prosperous time for us."

Enjoy your busy times, just as you do your quiet ones. Be grateful that you have so much work that you can hardly fit it all in, or that you have so many wonderful kids and so much time to spend with them at home when they're off from school that your house is bustling with energy. Your positive attitude toward busy times will rub off on everyone.

Once I was in a drugstore during the holidays, and I got a real kick out of watching the clerks in the photo department working. There were four of them behind a small counter—two at the cash registers and two bagging items—talking to customers, calling for price checks, and demonstrating watches and cameras. One of them was a manager, and his joyful attitude had clearly influenced his employees. He obviously loved working with people and making lots of holiday sales, and he had everyone joking and smiling.

I watched as a frustrated woman with a scowl on her face marched up to the register with a string of lights, half of them out of the box because she couldn't fit them back in. The manager chirped, "Let me guess—they're flashing, and you've tried everything to get them to stop so that you don't have to feel as if you're living in a cheap motel, right?" The woman suddenly switched from angry to amused, laughing as he pointed out to her which bulb to replace in order to get the string to stop flashing. Everyone around them began joking about flashing lights and little holiday annoyances. It was so busy that I must have waited in line ten minutes, but I didn't mind at all. Whether you're busy or waiting, doing a lot or doing nothing, you can create positive emotions.

Pressure to Make Decisions

When you're faced with making a decision and feel that you don't have enough time, or you're in a state of stress or extreme exhaustion, you're not going to be thinking clearly. Never make serious decisions when you're in a negative state of being—that is, stressed, impatient, tired, or depressed. Take the time to create feelings of relaxation, calm, and curiosity so that you can see all your options and choose the best one.

Stress stems from fear, which leads to additional challenges in your life, which could possibly affect your health, relationships, finances, and a number of other areas. When you give in to fear, you create the very thing you're afraid of. Don't become anxious about making the wrong decision, because then you'll be far more likely to do so. It's much better to take your time, use your Illuminators, and wait until you truly feel ready than to commit yourself when you're fearful.

Not making a choice *is* a choice, and it's often a good one. If you're focused on your goals, you're in touch with what you're thinking (rather than ignoring unsettling thoughts), you're working with your Destiny Switch to manage your emotions, and you're going to make good decisions when you need to. I've always found that being honest with myself about my feelings and thoughts, and working with my Illuminators to keep me on track with my goals, has resulted in sound decisions, and I've never regretted how much time it took me to make them.

In life, there will always be challenges. The Buddhists are right: Everything is impermanent. Change happens and you'll have to switch gears, but how you handle it is up to you. You can prepare yourself in advance to face adversity by learning to move yourself from a negative state of being to a positive one, and this will allow you to deal with challenges in a healthy way. You can also commit to developing the habit of maintaining a highly positive emotional state. In the next chapter, you'll learn how to create this program for yourself and tailor it to your goals and needs using the Switching Strategies you've already learned, your Illuminators, and a Destiny Planner.

∞∞∞

CHAPTER ELEVEN

Your Destiny Planner

No tool, no matter how powerful, can help you change your life if you don't use it. As I mentioned in the Introduction, many people read self-help books, become excited about the promise of improving their quality of life and creating happiness for themselves, and start to practice the program they've just learned but soon wander off the path to their goals. They have the resources they need, but they're locked away in a toolbox that's covered with dust and cobwebs. If you want to build your dream life, you've got to open the toolbox, take out the hammers and screwdrivers and levels, and start working!

It's very important to have a plan for the life you want to live and use the tools to help you co-create it with the help of the universe. Remember that your plan does *not* have to include the specifics about how and when your dreams will come true. The universe will attend to those details. When you're clear about what you want for yourself, you'll recognize opportunities when they appear and do what you need to do. For now, you simply have to know what you desire, use the contents of your emotional toolbox (the Illuminators and Switching Strategies), and get to work creating the emotional states that the universe will respond to in a positive way.

I find that the best way to avoid dabbling here and there, occasionally using an Illuminator or Switching Strategy and then forgetting that these tools are at your disposal, is to have a plan for practicing them on a daily basis. Don't get me wrong: Doing just one exercise in this book will help you get control over your Destiny Switch and start making positive changes in your life. If that's all you feel you can commit to today, that's okay, but I want you to ask yourself, *How important is it for me to achieve the life I deeply desire? How much do I want happiness, contentment, and abundance?* Don't let the demands of your daily life prevent you from investing your time and energy in working with your Destiny Switch. You can do these exercises in little blocks of time throughout the day, using your Switching Strategies whenever opportunities present themselves. Life is fast paced, but there are always plenty of opportunities to observe, decide, and switch. The benefits of slowing down, becoming aware, and practicing your Illuminators and Switching Strategies are enormous. The more effort you put forth to regularly use your tools, the sooner you and the universe will co-create the life of your dreams.

Whenever you see the results of the changes you've made in your emotional habits, you'll feel a burst of motivation and want to continue applying your tools to craft your destiny. However, if you let your mind wander to negative thoughts such as *I guess I just got lucky today* or *Well, that was great, but it probably won't happen again,* it will be as if you shut off the electricity—you'll be standing there in the dark, unaware that your tools are right next to you, ready to be used to build the life you want for yourself.

Every time you experience positive results from the Illuminators, stop for a second. Take a moment to be aware of what you just achieved. Experience the joy and pride, and say to yourself, *I did it!* If you chose to create love and curiosity during a conflict with someone and the result was that the two of you cleared up your misunderstanding, solved your problem, and went away feeling happy and connected, give yourself credit for your effort. You've just created peace, love, tranquility, joy, and connection and helped someone else do the same. How wonderful! Feel the joy, and be aware of just how powerful it was for you to create positivity in this situation. The more you're conscious of the results of following through on your commitment to raising the volume on positive emotions, the more motivated you'll be to continue doing it.

If you don't create positive emotions by using your Switching Strategies, or if you realize that you failed to look at your Goal Card today or listen to your Power Life Script, be aware of it. Don't judge or berate yourself when you find that you forgot or pushed aside your commitment to using your Illuminators and Switching Strategies.

Simply decide in that moment to work with them now. If you can't play the entire recording of your Power Life Script, listen to some of it. I have several copies of it so that I can hear it in my car, on my personal music player, and in my home. One of my clients listens to hers when she's preparing meals. Another client has Affirmations written on sticky notes that are posted next to the light switches in his house so that he remembers to say them every time he flips a light on or off. I post mine and my Goal Card in my bathroom, near the mirror—that way, every time I go in there, I use them.

If you're in the middle of a move, or you travel a lot and thus aren't in the same location every day, you can carry your reminders with you. A great way to record your Affirmations, goals, and Mission Statement is to print them on small index cards, which you can laminate with clear plastic and take with you in your purse or wallet. As I mentioned before, I carry my Goal Card in my eyeglass case because I know that several times a day I'll have to open it to do some reading—whether it's my e-mail or a menu in a restaurant—and when I do, I'll be able to access and use this Illuminator. It's often easier to create habits when you connect them to other habits, so if you regularly take a walk in the evening, for instance, make it a point to listen to your Power Life Script at the same time.

The busier you are and the more emotional challenges you face, the more important it is to follow through on your commitment to yourself to gain control of your Destiny Switch. If you feel that it's too time-consuming to sit and read through your Goal Card, Mission Statement, and Affirmations, why not try it and measure how long it takes? My guess is when you see how small an investment your Illuminators require, you'll be more motivated to use them. The payoff for putting in just 15 or 20 minutes a day to consciously create positive emotions is huge.

I've had clients who carried through on their personal promise to themselves to use the tools they possess, and I've worked with those who got distracted and stopped using them—and I can tell you that there's a big difference in the results that these two groups experience. If you want to manifest your goals, you have to create the positive emotions that will draw to you the circumstances you desire . . . it's that simple. If you merely recite Affirmations without truly feeling the words and envisioning yourself experiencing abundance and joy, you might as well be reading the phone book aloud. The ability to change your life comes from the power of love in your heart. Love connects you to your other positive emotions. It's the ultimate source of emotional fuel, so plug into it!

Creating and Using a Destiny Planner

Because it's very important to have a plan for using the Illuminators and Switching Strategies that will help you create the life you desire and it's crucial to be accountable to yourself so that you're aware when you're following the program and when your attention has strayed, I've created a Destiny Planner—a tool that will keep you on track. Use it every day and you'll see your life start to change in magical and wonderful ways.

In the following sections, I'll explain the pieces of the Destiny Planner and show you filled-out sample entries at the end of each one. (The sample is from someone who's looking to launch a new career but doesn't know what it is yet.) You can also download a blank Destiny Planner as a PDF document that you can print out, and you can even sign up for e-mail reminders to use it (visit **www.yourdestinyswitch.com**)

Whatever version of the Destiny Planner you use, make sure that you're able to take it with you wherever you go. If you have to travel or are away from your computer for an extended period, you'll still want to be able to fill out a page each day. Think about the most convenient way to use this tool in your daily life and when unexpected challenges come up. You might want to simplify your routine a little on those occasions when you're very short on time, but it's even better to commit to practicing your Illuminators every single day. They really don't take up much time, and many of them can be used anywhere.

Work with your Destiny Planner first thing in the morning, before you get involved with any of your regular activities, to set the tone for your day right away. At night, you can focus on being aware of the choices you made throughout the day and commit to doing a little better tomorrow. What's more, you can decide in the moment to feel gratitude, review your Goal Card, recite your Affirmations, and so on. Then you can check all those items off your list and go to bed.

On page 179, you'll find a reminder of what you need to do each day and evening of the week in order to follow this program. Note that you'll be using your Destiny Switch every day—that is, you'll be recording the levels of your four key emotions. Remember to pay attention to your feelings so that you can make the choice to switch into greater positivity. Whenever you think of it, use one of your Illuminators, most of which you can keep at hand wherever you go. Every time it occurs to you that you can create a positive emotion, go for it!

Step 1: Choose the Illuminators You Want to Work With

Review the Illuminators, explained earlier in the book, and choose which ones you're going to work with on a daily basis during the first week. Note that some are more time-consuming or involve greater planning—for example, the Life-of-Your-Dreams Experience takes a little forethought because you have to make sure that you'll be uninterrupted when using it, and you may want to record your Power Life Script as well as write it out. The sooner you create your Illuminators, the sooner you'll have a complete toolbox. Keep in mind, too, that each week you can choose a different set of Illuminators to work with.

At the beginning of the week, open your Destiny Planner and circle the Illuminators you plan to use over the next seven days. At the end of each day, you'll check off the ones you actually worked with. If you see that you've started to slip and not use all the Illuminators you selected, put down your Destiny Planner and try them right now! Why put off until tomorrow what you can do today?

Sample:

(Underline the Illuminators you choose to work with this week)	Day 1	Day 2	Day 3	Day 4	Day 5	Day 6	Day 7
	(Mark an x each day that you remember to use your Illuminator)						
Affirmations	x	x	x	x	x		x
Power Life Script							
Identity Board							
Mission Statement	x	x	x		x		x
Illumination Journal							
Daily Challenge	x	x			x		x
Daily Questions							
Touchstone Quotation	x	x	x	x	x	x	x
Goal Card	x	x	x	x	x	x	x
Life-of-Your-Dreams Experience							

Step 2: Focus on Your Four Key Emotions

Once you've decided which four key emotions you want to focus on in order to achieve your larger goals for your life, write them into the blank spaces on your Destiny Switch in the planner. You can use any of the emotions we've explored in this book, or you can focus on other ones. Your choice depends on what your goals and particular challenges are.

Each evening before you retire for the night, measure the level of your four emotions, and record them on your Destiny Switch. The next morning, review your Destiny Switch from the day before. If the levels on your four key emotions were high, commit yourself to maintaining them. If they were low or you feel that you can raise them higher, then vow to do that by the next evening when you revisit your Destiny Switch.

Sample:

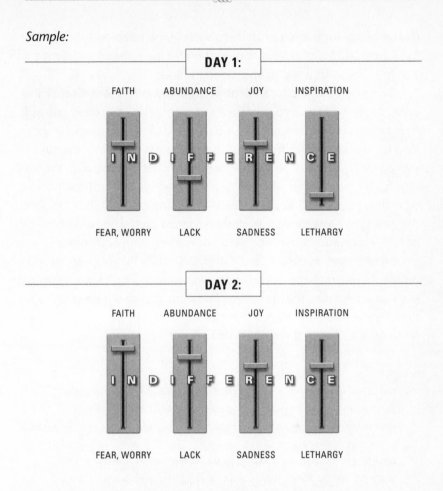

Step 3: Note Your Moments of Gratitude

When you feel thankful for all that you have, you attract even more love and abundance into your life. That's why it's very important to create moments of gratitude every day—for both the little and the big things. When you see your child again after work or school, connect to a feeling of gratitude. When you're walking down the street and spot a particularly beautiful cloud formation, be thankful. If you pass by a group of people who are laughing together, remember how much joy is in the world and feel grateful for love, happiness, and a good joke. As a freelancer, I'm able to plan my car trips to avoid rush hour most of the time, but occasionally I get stuck in traffic. When this happens, I feel gratitude for the opportunity to spend time listening to my uplifting Power Life Script. I have appreciation for my reliable, excellent car and for my health, wealth, and independence.

One way to create a moment of gratitude is to thank God or the universe for whatever you have, along with what you know you *will* have because you're manifesting it right now. Lately I've been thanking God for the wonderful house I'm in the process of selling, because it was a wonderful place to live and served Michel and me well. I thank God for the new owner who will love it as much as I have. I don't know who that person will be, as I haven't had any bids yet, but I'm sure that right now someone is manifesting this wonderful home for him- or herself, and we're in the process of connecting with each other.

So each day, as part of Step 3 in your Destiny Planner, record your moments of gratitude. If you didn't experience any, create them as soon as you realize this! However, knowing that you'll need to write down your moments of gratitude at night, you'll be more likely to remember to create them when you set out in the morning.

Sample:

Day 1: Forgot to feel grateful all day! Right now I feel grateful for a program that's going to help me manifest the life of my dreams, and I'm thankful for the love in my life.

Day 2: Felt grateful for my gourmet coffee in the morning. Felt grateful for the food on my table and for my wife, whom I love. Felt grateful that I have a reliable car to drive around town and that I found reasonably priced car insurance. Felt grateful for my Internet skills that allowed me to find good, cheap car insurance. Felt grateful for all my skills that will benefit me on the new job I'm manifesting.

Day 3: Felt grateful for my abundance, faith, confidence, health, and stamina.

Day 4: Said a prayer twice today: "Thank You, God, for my new job that's deeply rewarding and pays well yet has reasonable hours and lets me work outdoors sometimes"—I know that it's manifesting. Felt grateful for my community, which is helping me out in my search for work.

Day 5: Felt grateful for a day of pouring rain and high winds, because I pushed myself to spend my evening at my computer, researching my new career. Felt grateful for my shelter and safety.

Day 6: Felt grateful for the sunshine. Said a prayer thanking God for my great career. Felt grateful for my skills and creativity.

Day 7: Felt grateful that I have medicine to relieve the symptoms of the cold I caught. Felt grateful for my wife, who went out to buy it and gives me sympathy. Took the time to say my prayer of gratitude for my fantastic career that I'm manifesting.

Step 4: Record the Results of Creating Positive Emotions

Steps 4 and 5 are two of my favorites in the process of using your Destiny Planner, since they'll highlight the wonderful results you create by working with your Destiny Switch and balancing your emotions. When you complete them, you'll realize just how effective all of your Illuminators and Switching Strategies are, because you'll be looking at the evidence in black and white. In fact, every once in a while, I like to go back and look at what I've written in my Destiny Planner for these two steps because it helps me clearly see that I truly am creating my destiny by choosing positive emotions.

Do Step 4 every night. Remember back to points during the day when you shifted into positive emotions. Write a short description of the switch you made and what happened as a result. For example, did you feel better? Were you more energized? Also note the effect on anyone around you, no matter how subtle it was. When you create patience, for instance, you make it easier for your frustrated child or spouse to calm down and have faith that they'll solve their problem of the moment. When you create joy, you bring a smile to the face of the stranger you meet in the elevator. Don't overlook any of these magical moments of transformation. Write them down!

Sample:

> On Tuesday, I noticed I was feeling depressed and lethargic, and I switched off the TV I was watching, then went for a walk. I felt a little more energetic and hopeful and remembered to make a point of envisioning my business card saying just what I want it to. I felt faith that I'll manifest the business card. On Wednesday, I noticed that I was feeling disconnected. I chose to strike up a conversation with a landscaper I passed by, and I mentioned it was nice that he was able to work outdoors on such a sunny day. We talked a little—I felt connected to someone who enjoyed his job, and I started imagining what sort of environment I'd like to be in. I envisioned having sunlight streaming through the windows instead of being in a cubicle as I am now. I experienced what it would feel like, and I felt hopeful and abundant.

Step 5: Note When the Universe Responds

Every evening, record any evidence you saw during the day—no matter how small—that switching into positivity and creating uplifting emotions overall manifests what you desire and shines a light on your path. In contrast to Step 4, this is where you're going to pay attention to the more subtle clues that the universe is listening and responding to your heart's desire.

Pay close attention to those odd little "coincidences" that aren't really coincidences so much as signs that you're manifesting the life of your dreams. You may overhear an important piece of information or happen upon an idea that you investigate further and realize is a key to creating what you want for yourself. You might "accidentally" meet another person who is able to help you reach your goal or hook you up with someone else who can. When a wonderful event happens, note it under Step 5 in your Destiny Planner, and remind yourself of what you did in your life to make this situation occur.

For example, a client I work with has a freelance business, and she keeps a list of all of her customers and whether they came to her through ads, were referred via word of mouth, or were repeat clients. If she feels herself starting to worry about getting enough work to be able to reach her financial goals, she looks at her list and reconnects with a feeling of confidence and abundance. Whenever she receives an inquiry for a new project, she not only adds it to her list, but she notes it in her Destiny Planner under Step 5. She understands that by doing her job competently and with integrity—and by creating the positive emotions of enthusiasm, curiosity, and empathy—she's continually manifesting a solid customer base.

Remember, too, that the universe works in unusual and unexpected ways at times. Open yourself up to its creative methods of manifesting what you desire. You may feel lonely and yearn for a romantic partner and decide to help yourself switch into more positive emotions by attending a free jazz concert in the park, only to get there and realize that you're surrounded by happy couples. Everyone seems to have someone except you. You could validate your negative beliefs and create emotions of jealousy and sadness, or you could recognize that this is an opportunity to find love! Experience joy for these couples. Connect with your own feeling of harmony, and smile . . . be genuinely happy for them.

As you walk around, you'll be sending out a vibration that will attract another happy person. He or she might not show up tonight, but you make yourself attractive and available by creating this harmonious energy. You might find yourself cheerfully chatting with an individual who isn't a potential partner for you but who will somehow connect you to someone who *is* the right person. Don't forget about my friend Cheryl, who spread love and joy whenever she talked to her elderly neighbor, who responded by sending over her very handsome and available son to borrow a cup of sugar!

Make sure that you keep your eyes open for opportunities to manifest the life of your dreams. When you work with Steps 4 and 5 in your Destiny Planner each day, you'll see that your program for creating positivity really is working.

I love the movie *Under the Tuscan Sun,* in which Diane Lane plays a woman who tries to create the life of her dreams by leaving her cheating husband, taking a vacation in Italy, and impulsively buying a country villa that she falls in love with. She dreams of holding a wedding there and having children in her home and plenty of love. The road to her destiny is full of surprises: A promising relationship doesn't work out, and an old friend shows up at her door, seeking shelter after suffering a terrible emotional blow.

One day Lane's character happens to be hosting a beautiful wedding for a young couple she befriended, and she realizes that she's manifested a wedding at her villa, just as she'd hoped (it isn't *hers,* but it is a wedding). She looks over at her friend, who's playing with her daughter, and she realizes that she's manifested kids playing on her grounds (again, the little girl isn't hers, but there *is* a child). She sees the crowd of neighbors and friends surrounding her, and it dawns on her that she's found great love in many forms. Connecting with the feeling of bliss, she begins to walk around her splendid home—and discovers a good-looking, single man who's interested in getting to know her better.

This is what happens when you embrace positivity on a daily basis, regularly choosing to have faith and foster love. The picture you paint may be different from what you expected, but you definitely bring your dreams to life.

Sample:

> One sign that the universe is guiding me and helping me manifest what I desire is that I met someone who happens to do work that I've been considering, and he agreed to meet for coffee and talk about it. Another instance: When I was channel surfing, I came across a program on the history of baby-boomer toys; and this reminded me that I'd like to have a job where my work encourages people to feel happy, playful, and childlike. I don't have to settle for less!

Your Commitment to Yourself

I hope that you'll commit to using your planner every morning and night. Modify it in any way you wish to make it easier for you to incorporate into your life—and to keep things interesting. You may wish to rewrite your Goal Card and your Power Life Script again and again, modify your Daily Questions, or drop some Illuminators for a while and come back to them later. There are no rules, except: (1) to make every effort to complete your planner at the beginning of each week, filling in your goals and your Destiny Switch; and (2) to review your daily goals in the morning and record your results each night.

As you work with your Destiny Planner, you'll develop the habit of working with your Illuminators and using your Switching Strategies. You'll become increasingly aware of your power to manifest whatever you desire.

Recently, some friends of mine took a tour through a showcase home that had been decorated by several design firms as part of a charitable event to raise funds for breast cancer. Although my friends certainly didn't have enough money to buy a 22-room mansion overlooking a lake and they couldn't even afford the pricey furniture and draperies the designers had placed inside, they didn't choose to experience the house as a museum filled with opulent items they could never possess. If they had, they would have created a feeling of lack and separated themselves from their own dream homes. Instead, they connected with a sense of ownership and wealth as they walked through the home, asking questions of the guides, commenting on everything they loved, and talking among themselves about what they would do a little differently—fewer cushions on that sofa, a lighter color in the kitchen, and so on.

The women all pictured themselves living in this glorious mansion, and they also imagined using the decorating ideas in their own homes. One jotted down the color of paint she particularly liked. Another decided that she'd create a space in her own home for reading in the sunlight, just as the designers had done. Yet another was inspired to create a beautiful, removable skirt around her own pedestal sink. As they wandered through the many rooms, they created curiosity and enthusiasm (even as they helped raise money for a worthy cause). They left feeling a sense of connection to their own dream homes, and I know that they'll manifest what they desire with the help of a kind and loving universe that wants to see us live the lives of our dreams.

You, too, can start connecting with your imagination, faith, and joy, creating love and inspiration for yourself and spreading these wonderful positive emotions to everyone around you—from your best friend to the letter carrier. As you record the evidence that you're on the path of your dreams and in control of your Destiny Switch, you'll feel highly motivated to keep with your program for yourself. I know you're going to do it!

DESTINY PLANNER
WEEKLY CHECKLIST

(You can download a PDF of a blank one-month Destiny Planner from www.yourdestinyswitch.com.)

- **Day 1, morning:** Select four key emotions and write them down in your Destiny Planner. Make sure that your Illuminators are on hand and ready to use. Choose some of them to practice this week, and then immediately begin using them.

- **Day 1, daytime:** Work with your Illuminators and Switching Strategies whenever you think of them. Stay positive!

- **Day 1, evening:** Continue with your Illuminators. Fill in your Destiny Planner where you can, and use the opportunity to do anything you forgot (such as reviewing your Mission Statement or creating moments of gratitude). Go back over what you've written for the day. Experience a feeling of joy and self-love. Commit yourself to creating just as much, if not more, positivity tomorrow.

- **Days 2–7, morning:** Use the Illuminators you've chosen for this week.

- **Days 2–7, daytime:** Every time it occurs to you, use your Illuminators and Switching Strategies. Maintain your positive state!

- **Days 2–7, evening:** Work with your Illuminators further. Complete your Destiny Planner, and make sure to do anything that you forgot. Review what you've written for the day, and create the feeling of joy and self-love. Reaffirm your commitment to yourself to create just as much, if not more, positivity the next day.

RECOMMENDED READING

There are many wonderful books that can help you create positive thoughts and emotions and become more aware of your feelings. The following is a list of some of my favorites (alphabetical by author):

— *Three Magic Words* by U. S. Andersen (Chatsworth, California: Wilshire Book Company, 1980)

— *Your Invisible Power* by Genevieve Behrend (Camarillo, California: DeVorss & Company, 1921)

— *Simple Abundance* by Sarah Ban Breathnach (New York: Warner Books, 1995)

— *The Magic of Believing* by Claude M. Bristol (New York: Pocket Books, 1991)

— *Love* by Leo Buscaglia (New York: Ballantine Books, 1996)

— *The Success Principles* by Jack Canfield (New York: HarperCollins, 2005)

— The *Chicken Soup for the Soul* series by Jack Canfield and Mark Victor Hansen (Deerfield Beach, Florida: Health Communications)

— *Don't Sweat the Small Stuff . . . and it's all small stuff* by Richard Carlson, Ph.D. (New York: Hyperion, 1997)

— *Ageless Body, Timeless Mind* by Deepak Chopra, M.D. (New York: Harmony Books, 1994)

— *How to Know God* by Deepak Chopra, M.D. (New York: Harmony Books, 2000)

— *What You Think of Me Is None of My Business* by Terry Cole-Whittaker (New York: Jove Books, 1998)

— *Acres of Diamonds* by Russell H. Conwell (New York: Jove Books, 1978)

— *Anatomy of an Illness as Perceived by the Patient* by Norman Cousins (New York: W. W. Norton & Company, 2005)

— *Inspiration* by Dr. Wayne W. Dyer (Carlsbad, California: Hay House, 2006)

— *The Power of Intention* by Dr. Wayne W. Dyer (Carlsbad, California: Hay House, 2005)

— *Your Erroneous Zones* by Dr. Wayne W. Dyer (New York: Avon Books, 2001)

— *Your Sacred Self* by Dr. Wayne W. Dyer (New York: HarperCollins, 1996)

— *How to Think Like a Millionaire* by Mark Fisher, with Marc Allen (Novato, California: New World Library, 1998)

— *The Dark Side of the Light Chasers* by Debbie Ford (New York: Riverhead Books, 1999)

— *Man's Search for Ultimate Meaning* by Viktor E. Frankl (New York: Perseus Publishing, 2000)

— *Creative Visualization* by Shakti Gawain (Novato, California: New World Library, 2002)

— *Totally Fulfilled* by Dean Graziosi (New York: Waterside Publishing/ Visionary Publishing, 2006)

— *I'm OK—You're OK* by Thomas A. Harris, M.D. (New York: HarperCollins, 2004)

— *The Power Is Within You* by Louise L. Hay (Carlsbad, California: Hay House, 1991)

— *You Can Heal Your Life* by Louise L. Hay (Carlsbad, California: Hay House, 1984)

— *Ask and It Is Given* by Esther and Jerry Hicks (Carlsbad, California: Hay House, 2005)

— *Success Through a Positive Mental Attitude* by Napoleon Hill and W. Clement Stone (New York: Pocket Books, 1977)

— *Think and Grow Rich!* by Napoleon Hill (San Diego, California: Aventine Press, 2004)

— *Left to Tell* by Immaculée Ilibagiza, with Steve Erwin (Carlsbad, California: Hay House, 2006)

— *Love Is Letting Go of Fear* by Gerald G. Jampolsky, M.D. (Berkeley, California: Celestial Arts, 2004)

— *Out of Darkness into the Light* by Gerald G. Jampolsky, M.D. (New York: Bantam, 1990)

— *Feel the Fear and Do It Anyway* by Susan Jeffers (New York: Ballantine Books, 1988)

— *Unstoppable* by Cynthia Kersey (Naperville, Illinois: Sourcebooks, 1998)

— *Psycho-Cybernetics* by Maxwell Maltz, M.D., F.I.C.S. (New York: Pocket Books, 1989)

— Any book by Og Mandino

— *The Laws of Spirit* by Dan Millman (Tiburon, California: H J Kramer, 2001)

— *You Were Born Rich* by Bob Proctor (Scottsdale, Arizona: LifeSuccess Productions, 1997)

— *The Celestine Prophecy* by James Redfield (New York: Warner Books, 1997)

— *The Tenth Insight* by James Redfield (New York: Warner Books, 1998)

— *Nothing Is Impossible* by Christopher Reeve (New York: Ballantine Books, 2004)

— *The Disappearance of the Universe* by Gary R. Renard (Carlsbad, California: Hay House, 2004)

— *When God Winks* by SQuire Rushnell (New York: Atria Books, 2002)

— *When God Winks on Love* by SQuire Rushnell (New York: Atria Books, 2004)

— *The Magic of Thinking Big* by David J. Schwartz, Ph.D. (New York: Fireside, 1987)

— *The Writings of Florence Scovel Shinn* by Florence Scovel Shinn (Camarillo, California: DeVorss & Company, 1988)

— *Peace, Love & Healing* by Bernie S. Siegel, M.D. (New York: HarperCollins, 1990)

— *The Ten Commitments* by David Simon, M.D. (Deerfield Beach, Florida: Health Communications, 2006)

— *The Art of Spiritual Peacemaking* by James F. Twyman (Forres, Scotland: Findhorn Press, 2006)

— The *Conversations with God* series by Neale Donald Walsch

— *The Gift of Change* by Marianne Williamson (New York: HarperCollins, 2004)

— *A Woman's Worth* by Marianne Williamson (New York: Ballantine Books, 1994)

— *The Seat of the Soul* by Gary Zukav (New York: Fireside, 1989)

ACKNOWLEDGMENTS

Henry David Thoreau said, "Our truest life is when we are in dreams awake." So it is for me. My life is a "dream awake" because of my extraordinary friends, a loving and devoted family, and the most wonderful support anyone could ever ask for.

If I presume to share with you how to attract the life of your dreams, it is only because my own life has been altered by extraordinary people who have allowed me to be exposed to their great wisdom.

Bob Proctor gave me my introduction to this world of dreams awakening. He showed me that not only did I hold the key to my own prison house, but also that the door was never locked.

Neale Donald Walsch, through his exceptional talent and brilliant insights from the *Conversations with God* series, opened my eyes to a brand-new world of even greater possibilities.

To my faithful agents, Cathy Hemming and Stephen Hanselman of *LevelFive*Media, you are not only two of the most talented individuals in the entire book industry, you are my cherished friends. Without the two of you, these ideas would never have been created with the flow they have.

To Nancy Peske, who diligently worked with me to complete this project. I'm completely awed by your exceptional talent and deeply grateful for your dedication. You are an exceptionally gifted woman, filled with love, respect, and devotion.

To my wonderful friends at Hay House: Margarete Nielsen, who believed in this concept right from the beginning; Jacqui Clark, for encouraging me to be part of the Hay House family; Reid Tracy, for believing in me and the Destiny Switch concept; and Jill Kramer, for warmly welcoming me to Hay House.

To Debbie, for being an invaluable member of the Dynamic Destinies Inc. team; for your unflagging support during this entire project; and for your many years of loyalty, support, friendship, and caring.

To my mom, for your love and for the support and enthusiasm you express for my work. It warms my heart.

To my sister, Judy, for your unconditional support and all your valuable feedback during the final stages of writing this book. Your suggested revisions added an incredible amount of value to this book, and for that I'm very grateful.

To my son, Michel, whom I love unconditionally and who is my constant reminder to be loving, giving, playful, appreciative, and gentle.

And to my husband, Denis, for your complete love, support, devotion, gentleness, and inspiration. Thank you for being beside me and supporting me during the incredibly long days, late nights, and weekends. The God in me honors the God in you.

To all of you, I'm forever grateful.

∞∞∞

ABOUT THE AUTHOR

Peggy McColl is an internationally recognized expert in the area of destiny achievement whose purpose is to make a positive contribution to the lives of millions of others. She has been inspiring individuals, experts, professional athletes, and organizations to reach their potential for the past 25 years. She is the president and founder of Dynamic Destinies Inc., an organization committed to delivering sound principles for creating lasting and positive change.

Peggy lives in Quebec, Canada, with her son, Michel, and her husband, Denis. You can contact her at: **peggy@destinies.com** or through her Websites: **www.destinies.com** or **www.yourdestinyswitch.com**.

∞∞∞

NOTES

NOTES

NOTES

NOTES

NOTES

NOTES

NOTES